Someone Has to Say It:

The Hidden History of
How America Was Lost

As Told By:

Tom Kawczynski

Table of Contents

Prologue: The Truth Will Set You Free...From Your Employment

Once upon a time, not so long ago, I had what was in many ways my dream job. I had a peaceful town to call my own, and I was working for the welfare of about a thousand people up in western Maine. I was happy and the town was also, because we had come together as a community, building upon the bonds of trust that existed long before my arrival, but working intelligently to plan for a future where this small town could survive and prosper.

The insidious policies I had been working to achieve were the preservation of our medical center, improvements to the playground and docks at the park on the pond upon which Jackman sits, and saving money for our taxpayers while investing intelligently so we would be able to do more with less. Jackman remains a quiet town, wanting nothing more than to be apart from the world, but for a few days in January the world was turned upside down.

Just like the roaming eye of fire from those Lord of the Rings movies, a dark light cast a heavy shadow upon this hamlet when the media decided to send its emissaries to destroy me. The attack was swift, coordinated, deliberate, and deceitful, but I understood from the first moment that I was just a spectator in many ways to what was going to happen. As with so many other brave Americans who have dared to speak truth in an age where that is heresy, it was obvious I was about to be made an example.

Having been well trained to consider these questions with an honors degree from a very fancy college, but more importantly having watched these events play forward into the future in real time, I take the long view of history. Standard protocol is for most people to ignore the bigger trends around them and define their job and their existence narrowly, ignoring those problems which are too big to conceive or handle, and instead rearrange the deck chairs on the Titanic with deliberation and aplomb. I couldn't do that, because I could see certain problems coming and I liked to talk about them.

Using social media does not make me alone among Americans. While I keep my Facebook relatively inoffensive, I continue to be an active user in many other places, especially Gab (https://www.gab.ai/tomkawczynski) which is a unique place where people can and do speak freely, saying terrible and wonderful things in equal measure, but most importantly having real conversations about difficult issues. We talk about the future, about the past, about race, culture, people, war, and hope. And to be honest, like many others, I worry greatly for what is coming.

Some of my ideas are controversial. I think people matter and that we are more than just interchangeable parts. Culture takes years to cultivate and not every idea plays nicely with others. Race matters more than ever, and it's more than skin deep. Religions shouldn't be measured by the number of their adherents and their ability to intimidate, but rather for the decency of their ideas. People actually matter and we're more complicated than the anesthetized ideologies we're allowed to present ourselves as having. Take off the uniform for team red or team blue, and you might realize the referees ran off with the ball while we were arguing who won the game. Does anyone ever?

I want better and so I ask uncomfortable questions. Now, I knew I had left myself open to the sort of attack which came down upon me from above, because unlike many other Americans who dare only share their ideas under some alias, at least those whose views are right of center, I did so under my own name. All actions I undertook were on my free time, independent from any professional responsibilities which I exercised without fault and with courtesy and universal respect, but my crime wasn't what I did: It's what I thought. As we learn more each day, the punishment for thought crime is not to be thrown in jail, but rather to be branded and ostracized, and to be presented as the most wretched of villains. Depending upon your willingness to resist, you might find the resources of an entire nation used to dispatch what you say.

If having the national media attack the manager of a town of less than a thousand people with the full force and fury of their being seems like an odd overreaction, you're not alone. For the record, what I said is that a religion that marries off children, stones women for adultery, and sees beheading as a corrective might not be the best fit in America. I also said people might choose not to associate with people with whom they disagree, seeing freedom of thought and association as being implicit in freedom of speech, but the censors did not like that either. See, my crime was not that I was being impolite. Instead, my crime was that I spoke the truth.

Only after the fact and having been throttled by a machine so vast and so well-funded can I truly express my awe at how far the media, academia, and all their progressive allies go to suppress truth and freedom of speech. I'm certain they do this because they know people don't want what they are selling. Americans tire of forced diversity, of seeing their countrymen displaced by foreigners, and being told that even the most basic facts of nature must be denied. Americans everywhere tire of this predictable hypocrisy where everything is fine and good unless it happens to be white, male, rural, traditional, Christian, or straight. These latter you can deride without consequence.

As it happens, I'm all those things, and so the media decided to call me every name in the book: A racist, a bigot, a Nazi, and others. For my part, I tried to offer my own counter narrative, but except for a few alternative media outlets both locally and nationally to whom I am quite grateful, no such interplay of ideas was permitted to me. Any quote I would give would invariably fall under the headline: "Wicked Villain Denies His Inherent Awfulness". So, I stopped talking to them quickly, agreeing only to do live interviews which they predictably refused.

I want to take a moment to tell you a little about me, however, because I'm to be your narrator in a story much larger than my own. I'm not an angry person. I am motivated by love much more than hatred and wish no one – of any group – anything but the best success. I do believe ideas have consequences, obviously, and that you do more of disservice to someone by encouraging them to believe a pleasant delusion rather than a difficult truth. We lie too much to keep the peace, and there are ways to talk intelligently about hard subjects without resorting to autistic screeching.

I think Islam sucks. Sorry, but it doesn't belong in America. For those who believe that faith, there are many countries where they can find their fulfillment. While I recognize the First Amendment protects their right to worship and practice, that does not make it a good idea for our government to import Muslims by the bushel and drop them into communities where they do not belong as they have done up here in Maine and other places.

The difference isn't subtle, but I think people have lost the distinction between an idea that is merely allowed versus an idea that should be promoted as beneficial. I'm not arguing for a pogrom, but I am saying that instead of embracing the degeneracy du jour, we should oppose it and try to use both reason and ethics to encourage people to seek out a healthier belief structure. Another heresy, I know, but the connection between my eyes and my brain somehow keeps reaching my mouth, or at least my fingers as I type this.

I also think it's okay to be white. Actually, I think it's fantastic to be white. I am proud of who I am, where I came from and the people who came before me. I am proud to stand in a direct line with the many achievements my ancestors have amassed, and to carry that line into the future. I think white privilege is a load of crap put out there to persuade people to stop using common sense and instead allow guilt to cow them into submission. I know mistakes were made, but looking at the end results, we did pretty well.

Now, the media will tell you because I'm a white guy who is proud to be white that I am expressing some fundamental hatred toward people who are not like me. I never said that and don't feel that way. There seems to me nothing more natural than loving what you are, whatever that may be, as race, ethnicity, and heritage, are things about which we have no choice in what we are bestowed.

The funny thing about this area however is it might be the single greatest source of hypocrisy in the West today. Were I to have written about the rights of black people, or

Latino people, or any approved hyphen-based identity, I would probably be getting an award right now for my enlightened thinking. For the approved groups, identity is seen as a positive means of self-actualization and a way for groups to redress grievances. Why would it be fair for someone of African origin to seek money from the government for something people who looked vaguely like them experienced 100 years before they were born, but unfair for someone like me, whose family lived, toiled, and struggled here for 150 years to assert we belong here today?

Do I sound bitter? I'm not mad at people, but I reserve my anger for those who lie and twist words to play people against one another. That will come later, but I'm putting all my biases up front so you know how I think. If there's one thing I know, history is a narrative where facts are made to fit the conclusions, and I'd be insincere to suggest I'm immune to that. I just think my story holds up better.

Anyway, suffice it to say I'm white and I'm proud. I see the situation where people get special consideration for government financing, access to programs, and contracts as racist. Those exist – and they don't help the majority. Perversely, we aren't even allowed to talk about this, however, because our betters have decided that to talk about white issues is a form of racism. So, while every other group can organize to their benefit, all we can do is be glad to be permitted their sufferance while they undo all that our parents and the generations before them sweat and bled to build and be grateful for the opportunity to right their wrongs by giving away all our wealth, our control, and ultimately, even our population – as is happening in both America and Europe.

I don't like that, and though this part of history is still writing itself, there aren't any examples of a situation where the angry radicalized out-group treats the majority well when it assumes power. It seems to me a dangerous future awaits, which is why I live in a small town one hundred miles from anything, why I worked to make sure we were self-sufficient for all our people, and why I didn't give up my social media. I knew I could have made my future as safe as possible up here by having the personality of office furniture. I just also couldn't ignore what I saw.

So, this is why I was I fired. Legally speaking, my notice says I was terminated without cause on Tuesday, January 23, 2018. Only three weeks earlier, I had undergone an annual review which I passed with flying colors, earning a raise, and enjoying a convivial relationship with the Select Board which entrusted me to care for this town, a responsibility I took far more seriously than they did – being political animals as they were.

From the time the first story about me was printed on the Friday preceding my dismissal to the actual departure, they worked as fast as the law allowed with one goal in mind: To remove the pressure placed upon them from above. Never mind what the people wanted, or what they thought was right in terms of due process, freedom of speech, or even questioning what I said. Those were not appropriate because I now had a black label attached to me, and though I was watching years of effort disappear in smoke, I remain fascinated by how quickly this all happened.

I watched the pressure rise as one story gave way to hundreds of others, all saying the exact same thing, just with editors changing headlines to score points with their base and advance the approved narrative. Hooligans came to my town, an impressive four-hour drive, vandalizing property and putting up signs. Businesses were pilloried online, creating an impression of immense pressure to conform, and their combined forces suffocated any resistance. The Constitution didn't matter, the individual didn't matter, all that mattered was making the pressure disappear.

Knowing that, I was able to exact a sizable settlement from Jackman as the price of my departure, recognizing that was the best I could do. I don't blame the town for submitting because people here are good folk who just work, play, and pray, and they don't want to fight or negative attention. They hired someone like me, a harder and more difficult person, to take on this leadership challenge for them. Even though I am now free to say whatever I like, I'm here to continue that battle.

As I sat in the council chamber, with fifty people glaring at me trying to get me to break as I awaited the dismissal I knew would be coming, I was thinking only one thing: They messed with the wrong person. My parents were good people, and they taught me you must stand up for yourself, for the big ideas and for your own self-respect. My name was taken many places it never deserved to go, but they also left me one gift: A platform to speak truth to power.

So, with the end of my employment, here begins the more interesting story I wish to share with you, my readers. Have you ever wondered how America reached this point where it feels like we have no control of our own future? We now live in a place where a man can get fired just for pointing out obvious truths, for saying things our Founders wrote about and for which they are justly celebrated, or for just not submitting to what is essentially a very radical disruption of who and what we are.

America is not the politically correct bastion with 27 genders where the majority is the root of all evil. We did not prosper because we were unwilling to assert right from wrong, good from bad, healthy from sick, or because we feared social consequences. Those who tell these lies may be incredibly powerful in their ability to inflict pain, but please remember they must be because what they've created, over the past century or more, has to be artificially propped up with force, because it keeps you from living closer to reason and aligned with our more basic nature.

I want to tell you the story of how I ended up painted the bad guy for taking the same stances that would have been lauded not so long ago, and to tell this story of how the America we deserved was stolen from all of us.

Whether you believe me or not is for you to consider, but understand a larger reaction is building and neither you nor I am alone. We stand together with millions of others, quiet and waiting, as an awakening arises in America where we will come to decide what our future will be. To this point, only one side has been given the space to truly articulate their grievances, but I'm happy to offer this humble rebuttal on behalf of the voice of the unrepentant majority.

Introduction: The State Destroyed Traditional Authority to Take Power

The way we ended up in this situation where the world is upside down is no accident. Rather, it is the result of a series of actions spanning the last hundred plus years that saw the deliberate deconstruction of every source of authority and tradition in American life. Tremendous money, effort, and time were invested into numerous vectors of attack with the end outcome being an America that – in most ways beyond the superficial symbols we still laud – has been radically transformed, and not for the better in my opinion.

Why this happened and how such a project was concocted is a fascinating and extremely relevant story, and the obsession of many thinkers throughout the political spectrum. I invite you to consider your own speculation. Some view what happened as a series of coincidences in the search for greater liberty, the proverbial freedom from previous strictures and the happenstance outcome of individual battles pushing the nation in the direction of greater liberalization. Others instead see what was done as the concentrated effort of a few actors – whether they be individual or within certain groups – trying to reshape society to amass greater power or advantage for their cause.

History is messy because there are many contradictory actors and agendas all at work. I'm not going to try to offer you a narrative that removes that ambiguity because a lifetime in politics has taught me well such camouflage is essential to how change happens, and in how crises never go to waste. But what I will do is offer a very different telling of the events – factual and researchable – of key decisions that were made starting from 1910 forward. Within that narrative I will describe the impact these events had on our state and our society. What such analysis reveals is that as the state was built up, civil society was torn down, the family was attacked, and the individual was cast out to live in an atomized world. As the state grew in response to the financial interests who had such means to push the state in the direction they desired, it became an active participant in identity politics. It worked always to foment division and discord to gain its own strength as arbiter.

I never ended up writing my master's thesis in history, but consider this my informal offering for you, the public: For people with a radical program which ran directly counter to the wishes and traditions of the public of the western world, they could only undertake the state and social transformation they desired by destroying the key alternate structures of authority outside the state. Specifically, these are the family, the community, the church, and civil society. As people lost their moral compass due to having no trusted authority, people felt dislocated and uncertain, and to assuage such concerns, the people increasingly vested authority in a state which assumed all these functions and more in lieu of the traditional voluntary model provided previously through existing institutions.

We see this today as many families invest more money than time into child rearing, where the state subsidizes those who don't work to have children while giving relatively scant relief to those who do. Marriage is the institution that has always been at the heart of the family; an alliance to draw two families together for the benefit of their children and the perpetuation of the line. It has instead been derided and turned into a selfish self-righteous venial love accessible to anyone without responsibility. Not surprisingly, divorce also runs rampant as does having children out of wedlock.

The state also ruined the ability of the local community to sustain itself. Sucking all the oxygen out of the room with the massive taxes they collect at the Federal level and the administrative mandates with which every town, city, and state struggle to comply, our system removes choice from local and state governments to act as they wish. Instead, we are put into a titanic conflict where all the people are set against one another to try to force some common solution from above. It is an inefficient system contrary to the belief and intent upon which this republic was founded, and the driver for unending anger and recriminations. As the people who wanted to reshape the agenda were those most inclined to work within government, they were able to destroy any opposition which merely offered protest or tried to stop time at a moment worth conserving.

The reshaped agenda didn't help to conserve the churches either. The free speech of churches was punished, and the problems that were once actually solved through churches and community with care and dedication were supplanted by tax-supported programs. People stopped seeing the need to support their churches when their taxes were already handling the social welfare issues that churches previously addressed.

Now, we see those churches which remain play the game as well as any other actors and have become glorified nonprofits whose relevance only consists of their willingness to devote their now federally funded resources toward the transformation. A sad day has come to America when so many mainline denominations serve to place and import people of faiths diametrically opposed to Christianity, like Islam, and bring them into the flocks they're supposed to protect. Maybe that is why attendance has been trending downward for decades in all but the most strident congregations, but it's sad because we lost our moral voice – and now we seek to force politics to do that which it is ill-suited to accomplish.

The last piece is civil society which has also been turned against the majority. If you look at what academia, the media, entertainment, or their patrons in the nonprofit and government worlds espouse, they paint one picture of a beautiful world of tranquil coexistence. What they don't tell you, however, is such a world can only be built upon taking from the majority – destroying our values, displacing our people, and the perpetual payment of reparations to ever growing minority groups who are radicalized and weaponized as threats to maintain our compliance. They speak glowingly of tolerance, diversity, and progress, but if you dare to speak against this, the full force of this entire complex will destroy your name, your reputation, and your ability to live. We have freedom – to do what we are told and to be grateful.

Now, if you happen to be in a legally sanctioned out group, which for the purposes of this thesis we will strategically define as a group whose interest works to destroy the traditional sources of authority and tradition in America, you will be well-funded and exist beyond dispute. Media will promote your message, academia will bless your double standards, and entertainment will be used to bring the children whose parents are too busy to counteract their indoctrination into compliance. Race is one vector. Faith is another. Gender is a third. All these have in common one thing – not any connection to each other – but rather the willingness to serve as the means of destroying any resistance to the state and the reshaping of mankind here in America.

The people who conduct this agenda call it deconstructionism through intersectional activism. Because they have been able to deliver results, you can see feminists who still burn their bras making common cause with the Muslims who would subjugate them right back to the kitchen if they had power for but a season. These obvious contradictions and conflicts of interest should theoretically undercut their efforts, but conflicts are minimized because they're winning. Each is getting a portion of what they want because they all are taking from the same people: You and me.

They use political correctness as their weapon by reshaping language to force predetermined outcomes. They proscribe certain ideas, like asserting right from wrong, or the value of one group or one set of ideas against another to make it impossible for people not only to organize, but to even think against the agenda being promoted. We will talk about that more below, about how the medical field itself has been corrupted to weaponize mental health against what once was rightly considered normalcy, but the key point is they've delegitimized the ability for many people to even talk about their issues as such. If we can't talk publicly about what is happening, how can we have voice to shape our future in accordance with our values?

Politeness and tact are virtues in moderation. But the insidious thing about what has been and continues to be done is the agenda we face treats decency and forbearance as weakness. I know the biggest faux pas I committed was not in the logic of anything I've said, but in disrupting our constructed consensus by saying it. But that's just the point: We never say anything anymore, and ideas unspoken are not far from being ideas forgotten. For generations, we have laughed at the crazy ideas coming in from the radical extreme left, and yet have we not seen them come into practice first as a reluctant trickle only begging tolerance, and then a flood that soon asserts their right not to equality, but dominance?

Open your own eyes and consider what you see. I remember when gays just wanted to be treated as equal – now we see parades where degeneracy is marched down our declining streets and shop owners are sent to jail for not celebrating them. Muslims form their own neighborhoods now, enforcing their own laws quietly, with law enforcement treating them as above the law, knowing their own cities won't back them if they try to enforce the same standards to which you and I are subject. Black lives matter so much they kill cops and chant slogans against them, even as they already have legally gerrymandered seats in Congress, money for schools the majority cannot get, and special consideration after consideration. Can we ever give enough to these groups to make them content, for some supposed peace, or are we instead simply showing we have no belief in our own?

This book is about the destruction of beliefs we once held and ideas that were important to us. America once had itself a nation with the family at the center of life, belief that through reason and in concert with nature we could achieve anything, and pride as being heirs to Western civilization. Built of European heritage, and with individual liberty and responsibility in equal measure, we could achieve anything. We were bold, confident, creators, and exercised vision. But we let our flaws get turned into self-hatred, to guilt, and loathing.

Some express their dissatisfaction through seeking to undo all that built our great civilization. Many others have turned to apathy, total indifference to the process, and have been given ample distractions, whether through technology, narcotics, or otherwise to remove themselves from such concerns. Our current system is adaptable in that there is always another way to avoid confronting the issues, and the only real crime is working to preserve what was lost or replace it from within. For those who ask no questions, a comfortable life is assured, and even for those with talent and ability, we are promised there is enough money to have comfort for this lifetime.

It's a point that doesn't get covered enough in that we don't conceive of ourselves as having a future. Only today matters and a cult of youth is perpetually pushed. Now, we are not supposed to learn from our mistakes, not to look too closely at what has been done or is being done and are told just to enjoy our lives with naïve faith all will work out. We don't plan for our futures – money always seems to come around just enough that no one can fall off or out. We just take care of everyone, and make sure only the true evil can be identified: Those who wanted more.

There are many ways to define this struggle but consider me the voice of those who put quality over quantity, tradition over deconstruction, and the belief that we should strive for something better, for some greater unity in achievement, versus those who simply want to build a floor we all trample through congratulating ourselves for equality slightly above squalor. Because that is what we are given: A society based on equality as the highest value, especially without regard for truth, which can only ever achieve the lowest common denominator of the people who reside therein. And that is why you see high culture give way to high times, hip hop blared as brilliant music, and schools teaching children math that doesn't add up. No questions, no problems – the new American way.

Such a program did not happen overnight, and in the following chapters, I will share with you my personal understanding of how such a sorry state came to be. This history is not intended as a scholarly exegesis, so I won't be providing footnotes for every assertion I make. Such activity is how academics scrawl out pedantic livings, forever debating one another in one of those useless discourses where nothing of consequence is resolved and they seek mostly to bolster their own prospects through association with others. I will simply say I freely borrow from others, will give attribution where I remember the source of ideas, admit that others have had similar thoughts before, and take all blame for the inconvenient concepts I share as my own.

This is intended to be a popular history, accessible to everyone, and is a deliberately constructed narrative upon which I build my life now and exercise my own struggle to reclaim that which has been lost. As you read through, I ask you to consider the questions of not only how our traditions and freedom were taken away, but also why they should have been taken away in the first place? Having addressed these questions, we can then move onto the more pertinent questions of what do we want now, what are we willing to do to make that happen, and how do we position ourselves for the future?

A time of choosing will soon be at hand. The radicals from the far left have owned the agenda for a very long time, working through shadows and silence to come out into the light. They have effectively been unopposed. But people have begun to ask questions, like those posed in this book representing a decade of consideration and research, and an increasing number are coming together here in this late hour to resist. You might be told we are the terrible ones, the deplorables and reprehensible people, but what you might find is if you love America and want only to reclaim what we once had – not to force it to become something else – you're one of us.

Chapter 1: Bankers' Different Idea of Public Interest

There was a time in America when our government really couldn't do much, absent the sort of unifying public crisis where people logically banded together for a set period, because it didn't have access to all our wealth. Before 1913, the government could not collect income taxes and there was no central bank to lend at interest. Although there was disparity, the period between Reconstruction following the Civil War and leading up to World War I in 1914 was the first great building of America which happened because people had liberty, frontiers to explore, and were prosperous. We were increasingly a land of immigrants, but these were overwhelmingly people who came from Europe, who expressed the Christian faith, and who received no support save from whatever private charity and relatives already over here could muster. It was a hard place for some, but also fair and free.

People wonder how the government used to pay for things before they were taking large percentages from all the taxpayers. It turns out they were content to do more with less. The federal government issued bonds as needed on a case by case basis and used tariffs to fund government operations. The last point is important because one of the lies we have been consistently told for many decades is we need free and open markets to generate wealth. This is an invitation to the immigration thirsty population displacement agenda we've witnessed accelerate especially in the last 50 years. But there was a time when America was becoming a great industrial and economic power, based on production rather than finance, and because our government made a living off tariffs – designed to protect the American businessman at home at the same time it brought money from abroad.

Now, we see an inversion of that same relationship, as taxes become what businesses avoid. Our government protects business at the expense of the American people because they can buy elections. And if you think about it, when you have multi-billion-dollar budgets, putting five figures into a few Congressmen to ensure you get a piece of the action is a great return on investment. It will bankrupt the country eventually, as our debt now farcically sails past $20 trillion dollars. But that's what happens when you give government a blank check and you tell the people they can have whatever they want.

Until 1913, such largess would have been impossible to achieve because the money wasn't there. But government has a way of getting what it wants, and in this year, we see the beginning of the oligarchy that would eventually come to dominate America. The scam was that the policy makers in DC would be able to do whatever they desired, expanding government beyond the mandates of the Constitution, while slowly but ever in one direction growing toward the massive bureaucracy we have today. In exchange, the bankers would print the government as much money as they liked, or at least within the ever-loosening bonds of public acceptability, so long as they could make their share of the profits, a tidy sum that never shrinks as the government grows.

There is an exhaustive volume of literature on how this relationship evolved which I highly recommend as very relevant to today as the basic contours of this arrangement, much more so than voting or any other democratic practice, functionally shape our policy, politics, and economy. It was the ultimate sell-out in my opinion, engineered in secrecy including island meetings where everyone wore masks, and the media working in conjunction with banks to spread panic to induce legislation. So called yellow journalism had proven incredibly effective to instigate the Spanish-American War that netted Cuba and the Philippines, and it would become a staple of how subversive ideas were promoted and how the public interested was neglected.

It will come as no surprise to anyone that money makes the world go around. But most people have a strange calmness when it comes to taxation, accepting it as inevitable. They equally believe there has always been a central bank.

People hear about the Federal Reserve and their presumption is that it must be an agency that exists as part of the government to print money. Up until passage of the Federal Reserve Act of 1913, that responsibility was solely reserved to the US Treasury who would continue printing their own notes such as silver certificates for decades longer until 1971. But with the creation of this banking system, we now had what was a consortium of private banks, where large corporate banks own shares in this "public" entity, making dividends on the money printed. Where the previous United States Notes issued by the Treasury carried no interest, banks began charging the government for these bills we now exclusively use today.

If it sounds like a terrible scam, that's because it is. Those who argued for the Federal Reserve justified it based on protection against financial panics, and to have institutions capable of floating enough liquidity. But as the Great Depression would show just 14 years later, the Federal Reserve didn't have the capacity to accomplish its stated purposes.

The Federal Reserve was also supposed to keep control over the money supply to protect the integrity of the dollar and its value. Instead, what we have witnessed since the creation of these notes, is that their relative value as measured by their purchasing power has reduced fifty-fold. The best way to illustrate this might be to look at what things used to cost 100 years ago. We imagine things were cheaper in a simpler time, but why does that make any sense? If anything, the costs of production and distribution were much higher, but we get fooled by focusing too much on the numbers. What people need to understand is not that things cost more, but that our dollar continues buying less and less.

You can almost draw a straight line between the first tentative steps in fractional reserve banking, where banks lend multiples of what they own for every dollar they retain, and the quantitative easing of today where the printer runs pretty much non-stop to keep the economy afloat. The cost in inflation is terrible, where we consistently see prices escalate and sizes reduced. This happens because the Fed's real job is to keep a bubble floating. We get perpetual growth, an inherent impossibility, the bankers get rich, and all we have to do is ignore the fact that our money buys less.

It's easy to overlook this scheme when the government takes on all sorts of responsibilities for paying for the people's needs. But that was impossible to do in any systemic way until the government had the dedicated revenue required to undertake such a transformative mission, combined with a dedicated bureaucracy capable of bungling such actions. By legalizing income tax, the Sixteenth Amendment enabled the Fed, providing cover for the reduction in the value of money that was inevitable with allowing a private trust to print money. This combination created a mandate for the state to assume primacy over the citizen.

As many have surely observed, giving government a new authority very rarely leads to any reduction in how aggressively it uses its new powers. When the income tax amendment was passed Congress had discussed capping said tax at only 4% but decided to leave it alone because they had faith the American people would never allow huge taxation without rising in revolt. That may have been true during that particular generation but having opened the door to government being able to levy as much money as it wanted, their coffers would never close again.

Coming from the world of municipal budgets as well as having considerable private sector experience with budgeting, most institutions require you to identify your expenses before some external party will approve your expenditures. We all live within the constraints of such budgets, but have you ever noticed how those same rules don't really apply to the government? Every time you hear about some shutdown crisis, what they're really arguing about is who will agree to continue to print more money, even though it is now only debt backed by worthless fiat, but it is part of a game everyone plays – willingly or not. In later chapters, we'll talk more about how dollars were not only overprinted but detached from gold and silver. But for now, it's enough to point out that government was not given any such constraints on their own expenses beyond what they could convince the public to permit, and what they would vote for themselves. With the banks in partnership to launder funds, the scheme was set.

But obviously, the wealth to pay for this system had to come from somewhere. While money is created out of the vacuum in many ways, with increasing ease today as opposed to then, there still had to be collateral to float this system. And that came from the real wealth of the people of the United States, in the land they worked and possessed, and the assets they possessed which would. A change from a system where foreign markets through tariffs funded a humble and constitutional American government to a state where the people from that point forward be paying for the services which would sustain them is such a vast difference that it is almost hard to comprehend.

I often say we gave up our essential freedom in this decade because we gave away control over our own money. Americans didn't know this, and they certainly weren't alone, but we moved away from the contract where government exists to represent us to a system where government would now exist to manage us. Instead of them existing in accordance to our wishes, reliant upon the public will to work on the issue of the day, we now were given government by bureaucracy which would determine our best interests for us.

And we gave the privately owned federal reserve system the power to determine how America would evolve and what the government could and could not fund. The same people who Andrew Jackson had thrown out, who wanted to subvert Lincoln and his greenbacks, and who lived at the top of the social ladder were now invested with control of our entire economy. And as I know very well personally, when your economy is under the sway of others, your liberties become contingent upon meeting the economic necessities of your lifestyle.

We know what this sellout looks like because we saw the same thing repeat not so long ago. Remember the bailouts of Wall Street, where financiers became billionaires by infinitely reselling and repackaging mortgage loans on properties whose price had been artificially inflated by the very terms of the mortgages? That's what AIG did, why Bear Stearns went bankrupt, and how trillions disappeared – because they created fake wealth with real life consequences. The Republicans rushed to bolster business, and the great progressive Obama was happy to bail the big players out with your tax money. It must be nice to be the house and never lose.

Regular people work hard for their money, and perhaps because dollar bills are tangible paper, they believe there is a certain solidity to them. Money was once backed by specie or other hard assets, but now it is just paper. Money used to be scarce, but now it is essentially limitless save in what it purchases for you and the paycheck you likely struggle hard to attain. Money now gets created by all sorts of innovative institutions where financial instruments are piled on top of each other like a house of cards.

On some level, I think people know this, as certain practical folk keep supplies of useful things. They don't just keep gold or silver, but they also keep bullets, alcohol, food, and weaponry. The strange irony is as much as we build our entire lives around the dollars in our bank accounts and that pay our bills, I think almost everyone recognizes if order broke down for just a very short time, a few weeks, the paper would be worthless, and all that our society is built upon would collapse. We would revert to nature, and though that would be brutal, this example shows how money does a certain magic – it allows the creation of society upon some other basis than pragmatism.

Radical idealism requires the ability to buy off many people and to protect people from the otherwise inevitable outcomes of bad ideas. The banks and government began doing that, and their dreams were very large. They were larger than any dreams the American public would reasonably contemplate. But rather than constraining their dreams of what government could and would do to match its means and mandate, they instead looked hopefully toward a crisis that could change how people think.

Before Marx, there was Hegel and he presented the fulcrum by which the western world has been managed for the last hundred plus years. Two ideas are brought into conflict with one another: A thesis and its antithesis; an idea and the opposite. From these two options, a new synthesis is created which blends aspects of both, not necessarily in equal measure, and a new pathway forward is created to change how people think.

The thesis was America was a humble country that should keep to itself, honoring the admonition of Washington to avoid entangling alliances and foreign conflicts, and living within the Monroe Doctrine and as a nation apart. What began shifting the agenda was the antithesis that world is a dangerous place and we needed to build a bigger state to protect ourselves, because war would be coming. With the advent of World War I, many new syntheses would become possible, because not only do governments know how to take advantage of a crisis, but they're pretty good at embracing them to rally support and gain new powers.

Chapter 2: The First of Many Wars to End All Wars

A simple and timeless criterion serves well when analyzing history to see if the existing narrative is sensible or not. Who benefits?

In the preceding chapter, we talked about how the banks and the people who controlled them began taking control of America through the twin hydra of the Federal Reserve Act and the 16th Amendment, but while these actions created the legal authority to launch an unprecedented expansion of government into people's lives, having the ability to undertake such an invasion would not have been practical unless external threats scared people into surrendering more power to government.

As Randolph Bourne would rightly surmise just a few years later, "War is the health of the state" and war would soon be coming to America and the world, followed by the expansion of state power with almost frightful predictability.

It is often said that all wars are bankers' wars, and with good reason. If one makes their living upon lending capital and collecting from interest, then no human endeavor presents a greater opportunity to make money than armed conflict. Before the war begins, armaments must be amassed, factories built to construct these engines, and men must be brought into action. After the carnage, and even during the whole sorry duration, the torrents of destruction unleashed require rebuilding, and the lucrative opportunities for reconstruction constitute the ultimate way to cut past red tape to pure black profit sheets. The desperation of the cause allows banks to collateralize their interest and debts into influence and real assets, and the severity of the situation means the level of interest which can be assessed grows to match. Moreover, the citizens themselves become lenders, even lending an air of patriotism to the willingness to kill one another in what usually ends up as this pursuit of economic supremacy from which those fighting gain no benefit. This was largely the case with the imperial backdrop to World War I.

Considering how heavily American history focuses on World War II, which stemmed directly from the onerous war burdens placed upon the Germans by vengeful French, we have a strange lack of reflection into that first "War to End All Wars." I've long thought the reason this vital era doesn't get covered more thoughtfully is that the state which now educates us does not want us looking too thoroughly into its own construction.

America today basically accepts the idea we serve as policeman for the world and with that responsibility comes the requirement that we put billions or trillions into defense, a word that more accurately could be replaced by force projection. And we sacrifice our blood and treasure on many foreign shores to maintain a system we are told is for our benefit. Some call it free market capitalism, others democratic liberalism, but the truth is closer to banker internationalism, as the one most important institution in any nation will be the central bank. Any fixtures of international governance that exist as well are only democratic in a sham form. And we, as Americans, are their attack dogs. Patriotism is our whistle, and our love of country – what should be a great strength – is cannily turned into weakness.

The national sanctifying myth which supports this state of affairs is the pantomime battle of good versus evil, of which World War II is the best example in popular understanding. By promoting this idea, little wars can be managed more effectively, thereby preventing larger wars which would be cataclysmic. Leaving aside this gross and deliberate oversimplification of the later conflict, what matters here is the idea America must have war to secure peace. The Romans may have said if you would have peace, prepare for war, but it was the Americans who came to believe you must always have war to maintain peace.

Orwell would be proud of this inversion which he predicted, but if you stop and think how much wars impact our lives, how much power over our own nation we have invested in what we call the national security apparatus, what Eisenhower called the military-industrial complex, you can see our liberties have largely been sacrificed to the eternal vigilance of the ongoing war effort. Pick your flavor of Alphabet Soup: CIA, FBI, NSA, ATF, or whatever you like, and see how national security is the perfect reason to forever grow the state at the expense of the people.

What people don't know is how this started with World War I. Given the Federal Reserve System and the income tax, for the first time America possessed the financial means to conduct such a war. They promptly did so, as our new financial controllers did what any shrewd and amoral businessmen would do: they found the quickest means to conflict in order to maximize profit and gather debts, not just from within America, but also from the squabbling European powers.

Woodrow Wilson was elected and re-elected on a promise to the American people to keep us out of the so-called Great War. The vast majority of Americans supported this pledge, having zero desire to be caught up in the latest of what were a series of wars fought over imperial succession, control over foreign lands, and a race toward mobilization. Americans had no interest in the Old World, and whether Britain or Germany maintained supremacy in the North Sea and whose colonies succeeded better in Africa was not a matter of concern to our republic. We were focused on our faith, our families, and the challenges of industrialization.

Unfortunately for America, the state had different ideas. It seems like running government is a bit like having a sports car in the eyes of so many who end up holding that position. Having access to certain powers, the temptation to use them is an overwhelming human instinct, and it was no different with political leaders in our own country. A growing economic base and a potent navy had already shown success in the media ginned up adventure that was the Spanish-American War. This latter war earned us colonies in Cuba and the Philippines with whom we would struggle for a generation before ultimately releasing them to their own self-inflicted forms of misery.

The question of why we got dragged into World War I was an interesting one. Accepting the basic premise the state is comfortable with war as the ultimate justification for expanding its own authority, as occurred fairly recently with the ironically named Patriot Acts, the standard explanation deserves consideration.

The books that kids read in school tell them about how the sinking of the Lusitania, a civilian ship which was serving dual use of carrying munitions across the Atlantic to the Triple Entente (the French-Anglo-Russian Alliance) aggrieved the public. No doubt, the media screeched as hysterically as they do today, overlooking the culpability of those who would put weapons on a civilian ship and endanger passengers with legitimate war matériel. Then, following this indignity, the Zimmerman Telegram was produced, and following British Transcription, the American public was persuaded that Germany had sought to provoke Mexico into war with the United States, so we were pushed into the war to defend our own interests. Wilson would then introduce the idea of liberal internationalism, be the driving force behind the League of Nations, the failed predecessor of the United Nations, and through his Fourteen Points establish the idea of war for peace. Leaving aside the inconvenient fact the Europeans ignored his points and even the US Senate refused to ratify them, America still obtained victory, heightened prestige, and a larger state at the modest cost of hundreds of thousands of dead and Europe turned into a mess.

That's the version, with a few impolitic assertions of my own about the long-term consequences, of what is taught in schools. But after the war, I think we should return to this question about who would benefit. Between the twin demons of the war itself and the Spanish Flu which had an outbreak in 1917, a massive percentage of the population of Europe was lost. Germany lost its Kaiser, Russia lost its Tsar, France was devastated, the Middle East scattered in many different directions, and perhaps England came out for the better save for the many men lost. America gained nothing, but lost many good men and others suffered wounds. Our participation helped create the fertile ground from which both Nazi Germany and the Soviet Union would eventually arise, regimes rising in response to instability. We're told we could not have helped that outcome, as we acted for the good, but is that true?

Here is an alternative version of events. Germany was winning the war in the east as the Tsarist regime was incapable of meeting the needs of its people simultaneously with the sacrifices to the war effort. Seeing this, the British and their French allies needed fresh meat for the grinder. Absent that, they might have sued for peace as happened to resolve many other conflicts, and peace secured in 1916 or early 1917 would have seen some territorial adjustments, likely to Germany's favor, the Kaiser and Tsar remain on their thrones, and a more stable outcome. The flu could have potentially been averted or at least mitigated, and the ground would not have been seeded for the totalitarian regimes which would follow in the 1930's. While it would have been an irresolute outcome, lives would have been ultimately saved, and most importantly for Americans, none of our lives would have been lost beyond whatever few volunteers went to fight for either side.

The standard accepted explanation of why that didn't happen involves public outrage over double dealing from the Germans, and a promise that peace and democracy would prevail. It's a familiar refrain we've heard promised to us in Korea, Vietnam, Kuwait, Iraq, Afghanistan, and other places since that time. Isn't it funny how it never seems to happen, how democracy only sometimes takes, and the peace the emerges gives way to something worse? From the despot in North Korea to the psychopaths of ISIS, the track record of these interventions is scattered at best, and considering intelligent people know that war is a very blunt tool which does a poor job at sculpting out new paths from existing cultures, what would be an acceptable alternative?

The alternative version of events I favor clearly demonstrates who benefits, has a narrative that holds together far better than what is taught in school, and is also incredibly difficult to swallow. We have been taught – been indoctrinated – to stand against certain ideas and to never question certain people. Foremost among these proscriptions is that Americans are never to question Israel, much applauded as our supposed greatest ally, even though they have offered little blood and no treasure in our behalf. But I have the irritating habit of questioning what we are not allowed to question. An examination of the origins of Israel, the Zionist movement between Jews across nations that spawned that state, and how key actors behaved will inevitably spawn troubling questions.

In sharing these observations, my goal is not to slander any individual or to say an entire people is bad. Life is patently more complex than that, but I think it's equally true that any nation – a group of people who share a common identity and desire to assist one another – will logically work for their own interest even if to the detriment of others. How far a group will go to undercut the interests of others in such a pursuit is largely a matter of culture and morality, but within Zionism, the movement had been spawned within world Jewry – a people without a state – to use any and all means whereby their prominent citizens would realize a state of their own. All these assertions are a matter of public record in an unbroken line from Herzl until the creation of Israel, but the relationship between that effort and how America was used deserves scrutiny.

Palestine was part of the Turkish Ottoman Empire prior to World War I. The Turks were part of the Triple Alliance with Germany and Austria-Hungary. At that time, Egypt was a British holding, with the Suez Canal being a key lifeline of its Empire as the most direct sea lane to India. Though the Suez Canal had been secured from the Ottoman invasion by 1916, Palestine was invaded in 1917 by the United Kingdom with the assistance of Arab rebels and their own forces stationed in Egypt. Convincing the English to add more territory to their sprawling intercontinental empire was an easy sell, but with the Germans unbent and the Turks putting up considerable resistance at places like the Gallipoli Peninsula, the war had settled into a stalemate.

It's no secret wars are very expensive and with the impending collapse of the war effort of their Russian allies, Britain was facing the prospect of having to settle for an incomplete peace. Enter Lord Arthur Balfour.

We started by talking about how all wars are banker's wars, and in England, where the Bank of England was probably the wealthiest financial institution in the world outside of perhaps the Vatican, control had been exercised by the Rothschild family, a remarkable clan of Jewish bankers originating from the Amschel family of Frankfurt, Germany. As an aside, it's interesting to see how both the eventual European Central Bank spawned by the European

Union and the school of Cultural Marxism both originated from this same city of Frankfurt where the most powerful bankers held sway. Needless to say, Lord Lionel Rothschild held the ability to appropriate massive resources to help the British war effort, and when Foreign Secretary Arthur Balfour asked for financial support, the price was clear.

As made public in the Balfour Declaration of November 2, 1917, the United Kingdom committed itself to the establishment of a Zionist state in Palestine, even though the UK had no rights to Palestine at that time and had not yet expelled the Ottoman Empire from that territory. But such conversations had begun in earnest in 1916 or even earlier and were also used to bring America more firmly into the British orbit as prominent and prosperous people of influence such as Justice Brandeis pushed Wilson toward supporting the war effort. Reading between the lines, it's easy to see the price this declaration required was twofold: Financial support from the bankers for Britain's war effort and using their connections through the Zionist movement to get the United States into the war.

Let us return to Arthur Zimmerman now, who served as State Secretary of Foreign Affairs for Wilhelmine Germany. Considering Germany was already engaged in a two-front war, what possible reason would the Reich have for wanting to draw the United States into this conflict? It makes zero sense for Germany, and yet, we see this strange telegram sent through means that just invited interception which could only have one goal: To pull America into the war.

Speaking of the content of the infamous Zimmerman Telegram from January of 1917, concordant with when the Balfour Declaration was being hammered out, the telegram suggested that the Mexicans would be guaranteed their lost territories from the Mexican-American War from seventy years earlier if they were to enter into conflict with the United States. For their part, the Mexicans had shown no desire for another war with the United States as every such fight had ended poorly for them. The greatest aggression they undertook consisted of certain revolutionaries like Juarez occasionally raiding across thinly populated areas of the then largely empty southwest. The Germans would have known this, known how unlikely the Mexicans were to take up such an offer, and yet this telegram was sent through diplomatic channels where the odds of capture were likely.

Stranger still, when this telegram was first made public and the decryption was presented by the British to the Americans, Zimmerman decided to make public his endorsement of the telegram as genuine. Up until such accreditation, the American public discounted this missive as just an effort designed to provoke the unwanted war, but this man himself purposely pushed Germany into war with America, or at least created this situation. Why would he do that?

It made no sense for the Germans, but it made a lot of sense for a Zionist, and Zimmerman had a public record of expressing positive sentiments for the Jewish dream of a homeland back in what had been Judea. Getting America into the war and making Germany the target of a much-bolstered war effort was vital to realizing this dream. So, whether through promises made to bankers through loans, or key individuals undercutting the states where they lived for the nation they dreamed to bring into being, there's a compelling case to be made that Balfour, Zimmerman, Rothschild, and other Zionist allies were essential in bringing America into World War I.

Americans fought and died in WWI to realize a dream: We fought to realize the creation of a Jewish homeland, and in many ways when you look at American foreign policy in the Middle East, we have been fighting for that same cause ever since. I begrudge no people the right to seek a homeland for their people. Frankly, I wish we in America had the same clarity of vision. But what troubles me greatly is the extent to which some Jews appear willing to go to realize their dream and how oblivious Americans have been in giving their unqualified support.

Although this book is about American history primarily, we will wander as necessary to examine how other actors play in this story, and to tell the story of Zimmerman and World War I without talking about what happened to Russia would miss much of the story. Two threads intertwine here as we see the creation of the still-implacable enemy against which Americans would be called to sacrifice so much life and resources. And we will also see how Zimmerman not only helped the efforts in Palestine but served as part of a network that made sure the Bolsheviks, the original communists, were able to achieve dominance over the vast steppes of Russia.

What people don't realize is the Bolsheviks mostly were not Russian. They were Jewish emigres and intellectuals whom Zimmerman permitted to enter that country as the war was collapsing in the East.

Chapter 3: Our New Immortal Enemy, the Russians, Equally Screwed

Russia has a vast frontier, a distinctively Christian outlook on the world, and has always been on the periphery of Western Civilization, sharing certain features with the rest of Europe and having its own unique characteristics. In that, Russia is much like America and for the first 150 years of our existence, the Russians often served as allies to our fledgling republic. For instance, most people don't know this, but it was the Russian Pacific Fleet perched out toward San Francisco that helped dissuade the United Kingdom from involvement in our Civil War.

But Russia is also a very different country. Admitting that this simplification is a historical injustice, let's just say that at the beginning of World War I, Russia was a country in transition. It had always been a primarily agrarian country, but there was a growing middle class in at least some of the cities, populated largely by people who had come from elsewhere and tension between the farmers and the new urban populace had been ongoing since the Revolution of 1905 which led to the creation of the Duma, their Parliament, and the Stolypin Reforms designed to evolve the Tsarist system from absolute statism into something more akin to a constitutional monarchy.

Against this backdrop of internal turmoil, Russia was drawn into World War I by a series of entangling alliances including their traditional support for their Orthodox ally of Serbia. The war, however, did not go well for the Russians. Although they fought bravely enough, they were technologically less advanced than the Germans, and even more importantly, the regime started having problems providing food to their own people during the conflict. As these problems worsened, the ability of the state to endure began to collapse.

This all came to a head in 1917 when strikes that began in St. Petersburg, then the Russian capital, escalated to the point where the Tsar's authority was challenged so vigorously that Nicholas II abdicated. Not only did he abdicate, but he disbanded the Duma as well, which created a vacuum of authority in the Russian steppe. As the entities which had been formed to push the government aside, the Soviets (which means communes) in each locality started to take control in parallel with something called the Provisional Authority, an offshoot from the Duma which was more moderate.

Whereas the ancient regime had been traditional and conservative, the revolutionaries were Marxist and socially democratic in their leanings. Two main camps were in existence: The Mensheviks, or the more moderate branch, and the Bolsheviks, the more radical group who wanted to fully implement Marx's dictatorship of the proletariat.

When the Tsar was first pushed aside in May of 1917, more moderate voices were successful, but they made some fateful decisions. Many of their allies had been exiled and were living abroad like Lenin was in Switzerland or Trotsky in New York, and a general proclamation was made to allow all these radicals to return. Relevant to the story is that the majority of these people were not actually ethnically Russian, but instead were Jewish and had existed uncomfortably for many years within the traditional Orthodox rule of the Tsars.

In any case, the Soviets requested the permission of the German government, who was seeking to knock the Russians out of the war, to allow these figures to return through their territory. Zimmerman was very glad to allow passage, as they were fellow soldiers in the same Zionist cause which he believed, and reasonable justification could be given in that they could undercut the Russian war effort. In fact, they did far more than that.

The radicals who came back, led by a troika of Lenin, Zinoviev, and Kamenev, organized and radicalized the workers in the cities and took power in October of 1917. Just one day before national elections were to be held to elect a legitimate government, the Bolsheviks jumped past the Mensheviks and used the power of force, bolstered by an angry working class, to take control in the capital and then other cities. Within three years, they controlled the country.

Russia was no longer run by Russians, but predominantly by radicals who were Jewish, Marxist, Communist, and committed to stamping out traditional beliefs like Christianity and the family in favor of atheism for all but their own. Wealth would be reserved for a few, and the rest would work to see them enriched. Russia adopted a brute force solution to stealing the wealth of a country, something one could argue is also done here in America, though more elegantly through central banks running capitalism for the benefit of a few. But the similarities bear watching.

Russia has long been presented as our implacable enemy, through the trillions spent throughout the Cold War and decades of Hollywood propaganda. Even the fall of the Soviet Union in 1991 hasn't ended this suspicion of Russia as a convenient enemy which is pushed by the same yellow media today. But allow me to offer a different idea. Whether through force or finance, it seems the same global elites, consisting of many Jews but also plenty of Gentiles, controlled both. And owning both great nations in so many ways, the United States and Russia have been played off one another as the excuse for both nations exhausting men and great wealth competing against one another.

Americans, Russians, and all people usually desire peace and tranquility. It is only in the face of great danger they mobilize, and yet, we see how we have been set against each another to keep permanent standing militaries and the bureaucracy they require. Our Deep States are so massive now they control us beyond any hope of oversight or restraint. We can only hope and pray they serve our interest, despite overwhelming and troubling evidence they do not.

We are told communism and capitalism were the great foes of the last century, but both share certain commonalities: Both are materialist philosophies, obsessed with production and distribution, and equally destructive to the traditional nature of both the state and the family. Morality and spirituality are discarded in either the political crusade or the accumulation of wealth, atomizing people apart from one another in fear, suspicion, and the degradation of trust. This is the legacy of the West from the 20th Century, and if Soviet Russia was the hammer, America was just as much the anvil, if unwittingly so.

That might be a lot to swallow but let me put it in a different context. Most of us belong to one nation and think of the world through that lens, most likely as being Americans if you're reading this. Our loyalty is to our home, to our land, to our Constitution, and hopefully to one another. Yet, haven't you noticed how the elites of the world today do not share that same loyalty? We call them globalists because they are building institutions above and beyond the state and choose to live in their enclaves working for their own benefit rather than for the country from which their wealth derives. It's a curious thing in such a bipolar world that the emergent leaders should be globalist rather than Western.

Although different explanations can be proffered, the simplest explanation would be to look who had a global mindset the entire time, thinking of countries not as homes, but instead as resources to be used. Communists thought that way, as did corporatists who have in many ways taken over our own capitalist system, and when you look at the leadership, the coincidences become overwhelming. The Bolsheviks who ran the Soviet Union were as overwhelmingly Jewish as our media, academia, and financiers are today. And whether through usurious interest or through gulags, they amassed the wealth of the western world, and if you were to read through the ranks of the wealthy and globally influential, the degree to which they are disproportionately represented is beyond any possibility of chance.

During the 1910's, we lost control of our own fate in both Russia and America. And the two are intertwined. Do your own research and check how money was sent from New York financiers not to stop the October Revolution that brought communism to Russia, but instead to fund the fledgling regime. Check how churches were dispossessed while anti-hate laws were written making it a crime to call out Judaism. Or, if you're brave and stupid like I am, see what happens if you even suggest we should look into the role ethnicity plays in life, and how some groups are more allowed to look out for their own.

It's not what you're taught, and you're not even allowed to learn these things. The evidence is in plain sight, but people are so afraid of being called dirty names they would rather give complete power to people right in front of them. The means through which our submission is maintained would make any member of the old NKVD or KGB proud, because we've been taught being good citizens means not questioning anyone. We're told the reason is to be tolerant and accepting, and we are given a rainbow of diverse people, all set against each other, as the perfect distraction. But it is all designed to stop us from asking one question: Who has the money and the power?

We are taught through our history classes that power exists in some sort of vacuum, that trends simply occur through the ages and there is no actor behind what happens. The motive force of people disappears in this lovely narrative offered by the social justice warriors who argue we march culturally toward ever greater equality, even as it forces us to ignore truths. These truths are that our money purchases less, our governments control more, the majority is forced to surrender their values, and they increasingly find themselves marginalized and replaced. We make do with less, and if we look closely we will find the same Marxist ideology we spent years fighting abroad is quietly being imposed upon us here at home. The current political respite aside, we've seen the trajectory socially and economically move more to the left for the thirty plus years of my existence, and any opposition arising now is just a sign of the desperation that comes from a glimpse into our future.

They say past is prologue, and so let us look more closely at the Soviet Union as the example of what the globalists plan for us should they succeed. The Party Elite will continue to do quite well, but we will work even longer hours but be permitted to keep still less of what we earn. Of course, we will have the option of whatever vices we like, to move beyond any conception of God to feeling good, where drugs and distraction will be welcome. But politics will be off limits. Even speaking out against what is happening will cost you your job, your name, and your economic ability to exist.

Before you say the First Amendment would prevent such action in America, let me assure you it does not. If your views do not conform with what is politically correct, it is not only socially acceptable but will be encouraged for you to be ostracized and fired. Your friends will turn against you as surely as they would for any secret police, and in so many ways, our situation is more dangerous because we're self-inflicting these wounds without anything more than the threat of taking away our toys and saying mean words. All because some very powerful and wealthy people don't want certain things mentioned.

We might not have gulags. We make a few dollars to work. But how much can we really change with what we earn? Two parents work now to make what one did just two generations ago. We are told that technology makes everything cheaper and more productive, yet costs continue to rise. Capitalism defeated communism, perhaps, but was it because we ended up being better at imprisoning ourselves than anyone could have done by force? After all, we like the idea of freedom, and we like imagining no one has control over us, and a powerful belief can get enough support that people follow it without regard to its veracity.

That's why Marxism evolved into culture from economics. The economic numbers of taking from those who work and giving to those who don't have failed miserably in the Soviet Union and every other country where it has been tried. People learn the scam quickly and learn to do the minimum while they either sell out or work the black market. But the idea that everyone should be taken care of...well that is harder to destroy, and so that became the rallying cry. In an unjust world, the Marxists would offer fairness for the downtrodden and they would give as much as required, taking it from whomever they could, to find the equality they couldn't with their economics. The burn is slower this way and the majority is much more easily goaded into agreement, but it's just as doomed to fail.

No two men are equal. No two groups are equal. No two ideas are equal. Reason allows us to judge between their respective merits. But we have been trained to suppress our own ability to think and discern in favor of following dogma. We are told to uncritically accept that race is fake, gender is a construction, and freedom is absolution. We live as if these patent untruths are real and wonder why everything we build upon them fails. We like the lie because we desire equality, even at the cost of reality.

There's always a price in living a lie. The Russians as well as all the other people who lived under the Soviet regimes of Lenin, Stalin, and others have learned that. Generations lived in poverty, squalor, fear, and subjugation, and tens of millions were killed. If you add the other Communist states, that number rises into the hundreds of millions of people whose lives were sacrificed in the hunt for some absolute truth and utopia of justice and equality.

Such a vision has never been American. Our scope was always smaller, more decent, humbler, and achievable. It was about families, living the life of the spirit, finding means enough to sustain ourselves with some prosperity, and placing achievement over equality. It is why we have survived the worst of what tainted the Old World. But in our time, we now face the choice whether we will follow our leaders as the Russians did in the descent toward illusory equality, or if we instead activate our reason and engage our passion to look for a better future. We might not find perfect justice, but we can find a better life rooted in truth and our own heritage.

Russia is learning that now. A generation removed from the Red Menace, look how Marxism is shunned by most and how the Orthodox Church has returned. Consider how families are starting to value children beyond money or status, and how life itself is emerging. Life is a terrible and dangerous thing, competitive and grizzly, and yet doesn't it overwhelm the stolid sameness of death?

Russia is not our enemy, but it is our warning. It is what America will become if we repeat the mistakes of Marxism, and if we give in to the censors of political correctness. When we allow the secret police to have more power than the people, and we surrender our free will and the means to use it, like our Second Amendment, what is to stop those in charge from using all the power they can to make sure they stay in control?

I believe in one basic conspiracy theory in life. Those in power will do whatever it takes to stay there. We see ample evidence of this reality, but we hesitate to critically examine either our own past or present under such scrutiny, because we tell ourselves (and are repeatedly told) we are masters of our own fate, but you must determine how true that statement is. My unhappy task as narrator is to share the story where few of our choices have really been our own for some time, and as we advance past the bitterness of the Great War, to consider now how the good can be used to separate us even more easily than the bad.

Chapter 4: To Implement a Solution, First Create a Problem: Prohibition

Think about a movie for a second. A film can cover decades in the course of only several hours because it skips over the many hours of our lives where what happens is incredibly mundane. Sleep takes up a quarter of our time or more, and unremarkable but necessary efforts like eating, bathing, and other daily monotony consume much of our attention. They're not very interesting, but if you think more deeply, so much of what we become stems from what happens in between. History is no different.

We tend to look at great events for how they shift trajectories and how they change what we seek to accomplish. Using trauma to learn, react and persevere is hardwired into our system. Such psychology is often used against our interests by those who understand these tendencies far more clearly than they admit. They use our predictable reactions to trauma in order to induce us to surrender liberty in exchange for security. Such actions are inevitable, but for all the control they take, even such planning would prove very limited if there were no way to reach people during those in-between times when things aren't happening.

For the purposes of our survey, the 1920's represent such a time. Known as the Roaring 20's, these were a time of growth and free expression that followed the harder times of the war period. An analog for the far more destructive 1960's, we saw a liberation of sexuality in many ways, and the perverse spread of alcoholism under Prohibition. More importantly, as we shifted from agrarian life toward urban or suburban existence, we saw how comforts are used to induce people to give up their traditional beliefs, finding themselves instead on their own.

It is an entirely fair and unanswerable question to what extent technology and urbanization are responsible for individuals breaking away from the traditions of society which were previously needed to sustain them. Many would make the case such drift was inevitable, and to a certain extent, that seems likely to be true. But the particulars are interesting, because as Americans left the farm life, moving toward the city represented a number of opportunities. Yet, does it not seem that at every interval, today as then, the move was against that which brought us together?

Prohibition is a fascinating experiment. It baffles one today to think the whole country might have been willing to give up alcohol, which would seem a clear rebuke to my argument the 20's were designed to erode morality. After all, drunkenness was certainly not a new vice having several hundred years to negatively impact many lives. Yet, it's a curious thing the government would go so far as to enact the 18th Amendment to constrain these vices, and even more curious that it should fail so spectacularly that it is the sole proscription of our Constitution which would ever be explicitly repealed.

Why did it happen? Looking back, you can find pictures of a group called the Women's Temperance League along with others marching around sternly in opposition to what was happening in their society. I have zero doubt as to their genuine concern, but as will become a recurring trend, when activist groups are successful, it's worth taking at least a moment to look beyond their own ideology to see who is funding them.

In the case of temperance advocates, you find they were incredibly generously funded by magnates of the oil industry including John Rockefeller. Still reeling over the Sherman Antitrust Act split up of the Standard Oil monopoly, gasoline companies not only had to contend with the government seeking to split up their potential monopolies, but also that farmers could use grain alcohol as an alternative fuel source for the quickly rising automobile industry.

Another core belief of mine is those who devote their lives to profit-making trend strongly toward becoming amoral. Corporations are set up for explicitly that purpose and are designed to exist as independent legal actors protecting those who run them from the liability, responsibility and public scrutiny so long as they meet government requirements. With this understanding and many painfully illustrative examples to draw upon, it's easy to see how the growth of government which shot up due to the revenue collecting abilities forged in the previous decade would lead quickly to business trying to buy government to do its bidding.

Prohibition, seen from that light, is the first major effort to buy a policy. Grain alcohol was essentially made criminal so that gasoline would have a monopoly. The public would never go for government limiting their right to have alternative fuel sources, but they might just go for a plan which sought to eradicate some vice from their society. In this case, the effort was not explicitly connected, but the government would favor such action because it met their need to look good, or at least look like they're doing something. This reveals how they would be overly sensitive to the appearance of public pressure. Just as importantly, prohibition empowered government to have new authorities, and thus began the rise of the FBI as Federal Police.

Cynically speaking, one could comment the government created a problem which did not exist by making liquor illegal. The oil industry liked it because it allowed them to create a functionally unassailable monopoly which exists to this day, because even after prohibition was rescinded, an entire national infrastructure had been built on gasoline as the single fuel source for passenger cars. Not only did legitimate industry like it, but a new thing was learned very clearly: if people wanted to do things outside the boundaries of what was acceptable, making something popular illegal was a great way to fund certain projects and to keep the tension in society needed to push government.

Black markets are a part of any society, but as government becomes more demanding, they emerge most clearly to satisfy consumer demand. With the speakeasies of the 20's, we saw the first cartels which would meet those needs, bringing booze from Canada and stills set up out in the county to satisfy those clients. Because this was illegal, muscle became part of the operation and we saw the first major crime syndicates take root in America.

There's an important lesson in this example that those of us who decry degeneracy have to consider very carefully in how our own impulses to encourage forthright behavior can sometimes create something far worse. Once the institution of the mob was created, how long would it be before the government started snooping into all our lives? Once alcohol was freely permitted, how predictable was it the people who had made so much money would choose to engage in other crimes and to push other even more dangerous goods? Those struggles with drugs continue even more painfully today.

It's another demonstration of Hegel in action, how a problem suggests its own solution. It's the recurring American problem throughout the 20th Century: Government tries to solve one issue, usually at the behest of an insincere actor, and creates several other problems in its wake. Invariably, government gets bigger, business makes a deal with government to share control in exchange for a cut of whatever profits, and the people end up further removed from their representatives.

Although it would pick up greater speed and urgency during FDR, other cartels also formed during this period. One cartel that people don't regularly think of is the American Medical Association. Their branding is such you would never realize that they represent no more than a third of the doctors, but the reason they were founded was to shift away from the longstanding practice of naturopathy – traditional home-based medicine which included many natural remedies toward the currently mandated allopathy – drugs and state regulation with strict controls that give them a legal monopoly.

Fast forward to today. Patients are not allowed to make medical choices, and big pharmaceutical companies promise a pill to treat every symptom and discomfort, though they are strangely lacking when it comes to discovering cures. What was first presented as but one viable choice among many has, through contact with government and the promises of experts, grown to constrain the whole country into a single vision of what constitutes acceptable health care. Although many false practices were surely followed by people in earlier days in America, it's unarguable that we have fewer choices today about health than we once did. It is just as true that our health care system is now much more driven by money than health. We will revisit this later in some detail.

I have spent much time talking about institutional actors because I want you to see how the state claws control away from the people one act at a time by supposedly attempting to satisfy our needs. But instead it creates an edifice whereby control can be taken by certain actors, usually those with the most money or influence. Therefore, we must perpetually ask who owns whom, looking at who pays for policies, and always understanding our society is not just a function of laws and politics, but much more so of business, culture, finance, and how these are used to shift our opinions of what is acceptable.

The people who went to the speakeasy back in the 1920's and ran around with flapper girls did not often abandon their families and were likely only seeking to have fun. But as they devoted themselves to having a good time, the idea of leisure as the center of American life became prevalent and some people liked that path. If alcohol provided the means to enjoy that life, and money had to flow in certain directions to obtain such bliss, that would be okay as a new means to explore self-expression. After all, what could be a more American value than freedom?

The leftist narrative basically sees the 20th century as an arc where increasing economic ability allows for individual freedom to act and find new means of cultural expression and individual autonomy. They're not wrong in observing this happened, but what they never question is what price was exacted when instead of serving as mothers and fathers, people decided to pursue their own happiness without any regard to the well-being of the next generation.

Let's shift their attitude to today: How many people do we see proclaim fidelity to themselves as their highest value? Leaving aside the obvious point that such a value system is ever-changing, consider how we have rationalized materialistic selfishness as the highest value and as our form of relief from the world. We have paid a high cost by giving government the responsibility to handle so many aspects of our lives, so we do not have to assume these responsibilities. Even such basic roles as feeding ourselves, raising our children, and the like are now covered if asked, and what has having such freedom done to us? We can now do anything, accept anyone, and just live our imaginations.

But who is running the ship? As we chase these selfish dreams, which most often turn out to be our most basic vices for sex, security, and validation, have we considered asking where is our civilization is going? We dreamed of the stars and what we could do together, but now we spend billions just to get along. We are told this is so we will have no suffering, but is it not equally true that we can now offer no vision? We chose comfort, and it seems that through that choice we have also decided that mediocrity is good enough for everyone, a goal we all can achieve together.

It's weird how capitalism and communism ultimately come to the same conclusion until you understand that both are materialist philosophies who believe man's quest for meaning can be solved by having a certain amount of stuff. One system operates on fear whereas the other uses greed, but both encourage vice and in their process of isolating individuals from one another, both empower the state. Only through the spirit to accomplish more, rooted in the love and altruism of the greater family has this ever been resisted, and this purpose beyond materialism has been shattered.

We choose to be so individualistic that we cannot work with one another. In this we find the slow decline of decadence, and when we look at the 20's, we can see the appeal. We can see how people didn't go to Church so much, and maybe the daughter ran away from the farm and the responsibility to care for her grandmother who had been there for her. We see how families and duties are not so fun. It didn't happen then, but the same mentality underwrites women who choose to work rather than raise a child.

The 60's are where we will go into the full depth of the consequences of the various cultural revolutions and gain a clear understanding of what Cultural Marxism did to America. But the test run of the 1920's is a glimpse into just how long this battle has been fought, and it shows you just how long this struggle has been simmering.

The difference, however, is that the end of the 1920's with the Great Depression erased these ideas. That misery served as a reality check, showing people that our basic needs don't expire when individuals are all on their own, just living the good life. The Great Depression built a hard generation and perhaps a better one, who knew how to survive and who understood that planning for problems and maintaining social glue is a necessity for civilization as we cannot continue to just hope government will bail us out.

During the Great Depression, the very thing the Federal Reserve was supposedly created to prevent happened – and our economy was destroyed. Nobody talks about that, nor do they talk about how a war was needed to end that depression, which resulted in a further erosion of our liberties and the eventual creation of the permanent police state – a national security apparatus which would dwarf the nascent FBI. We are told these things just happened, but it's funny how crises are so reliably cyclical and how those who run our governments use them to bolster their power and control.

While World War II reset the economy to end the Great Depression, while it was ongoing, the depression also provided the opportunity for the next President, Franklin Delano Roosevelt to redefine freedom itself and give government more power than had ever been imagined before to shape and control our lives. In despair, the American people entered the 30's demanding any solution to make the pain stop.

Chapter 5: The New Deal Sucks – America Learns Dependency

Before I was a Town Manager, I had been both a candidate and a campaign manager working from the political side. In fact, one of the reasons I believe I was hired to serve up here in Maine for the town is because I was willing to work not just the policy angle but understood clearly that sometimes politics is needed to change an agenda. There is a strange lie that permeates bureaucracy everywhere that they are somehow apolitical, free from the bias all humans express, and which is almost always untrue.

The bias here is simple: People who think government does useful things tend to be more likely to be involved with government to see such solutions as helpful rather than harmful. It's no accident the vast majority of my peers stumbled over themselves to deride me because the overwhelming majority of those who both run local government offices and who work therein lean left. Because they are the ones who play, it's no accident policy takes on the flavors they desire.

I was working to change that in subtle and quiet ways. Instead of using stories that employed guilt and empathy to accentuate resource distribution to foreigners, I instead emphasized, as popular sovereignty dictates, that our governments should look out for our own people. My ideology was at the heart of why I was effective at my work, because I put my own people first with clear and unapologetic lucidity, and I know that is a virtue that some would consider sinful.

The organizers on the radical left have long understood the lesson that the path to political power runs through relating to the people, at least rhetorically, and being utterly unapologetic about using government in every way possible to accomplish their ends. We see how they have ignored the Constitution for years, preferring instead to promote activist judges who torture the law into definitions clearly contrary to the expressed written intent of the document. And we see how social programs get funded and money percolates into our system both directly and indirectly to promote their form of social engineering.

These ideas had existed for many years beforehand, but they found their fulfillment in Franklin Delano Roosevelt's New Deal. In short, he promised everything to everyone, a fundamental transformation of the American system which was only possible because of the severity of the ongoing Great Depression whose roots we previously touched upon. He promised to rein in the banks, even though bankers were also his source of funding and support in the usual urban centers. He promised that wherever industry had failed, government would intervene to take care of the people directly.

Cleverly, he packaged his agenda of socialist ideals as freedoms, including old saws like speech and worship, but he added freedom from want and freedom from fear. The first two had long been established as natural rights inherent in our being that only disappeared when government or other actors used violence or the threat of penalty to restrain them. But so-called freedom from want was a very different animal: It legitimized this idea the government existed to care for the direct needs of the people: The welfare state.

Before the 1910's, the Federal Government lacked the ability to even suggest such an agenda because there was no money available for them to legally pay for such a program. But FDR took the opportunity which the Republicans had largely avoided through the 1920's, and created numerous programs designed to ensure the government was involved with our lives from cradle to grave, the most famous of which is Social Security.

Originally designed as a pension supplement program, it has now blossomed into the sole source of retirement for many impoverished Americans, sustenance for poor and disabled people, and an entitlement which annually consumes an ever-greater portion of government funds. Put in technical jargon, it is an unfunded liability that is politically sacrosanct, and so more of our wealth is trapped in a program which is inefficient and has expanded far beyond our reach.

Unlike some on the right, I don't believe we benefit from attacking the poor, especially today as they are often misled by a poor education system, lack of parents, and deceptive media. My experience in politics has shown me that once a policy or program exists, someone will use it, and that's true with the welfare state. But two thoughts which are important do emerge.

The first is that once Americans accept that a given problem is government's responsibility, it changes how we think about those issues. We once dealt with helping our poor as a community responsibility driven by genuine human concern, and we looked to church and charity to step in to cover the difference., But now that it is accepted as a governmental responsibility, the programs are driven by mandate and we have absolved ourselves of any concern. The left calls this kindness, and the right usually calls it a tax burden, but is it not more truly a sort of bland forgetfulness? We allowed government to undertake a basic human task, and as a result we stopped caring for one another, stopped investing the time to help each other, and we became separated just that little bit more.

Our consciences receive instant absolution as we assert that the government has the problem solved, but now we have made social planning a function of the state where it used to be a choice of the individual. Having delegated such authority away, is it any surprise that institutions like the Church and the community partners would begin to decline and disappear? We see a clear analog in overtly socialist countries where the state simply removes such intermediary actors, but here in America, it has been a slow and gradual replacement. Instead of public works motivated by fellowship and charity, these are now assigned as tax burdens and obligations. Warmth has become a cold bureaucracy, and kindness has been displaced by burden.

Offering no such consideration to politicians who know precisely what they're doing when they usurp authority from the people, it's not hard to understand why the happy rhetoric of helping people would prove inspirational. In desperate times, and with a rapidly changing electorate with women now having the ability to vote, the idea that the state could help for a time must have sounded like a great kindness. And indeed, there might even be times it should be considered, but what is never mentioned is that such help comes with a devastating social price in that every time we become responsible for less, we also become that much more disconnected.

It's easier to see the results of those fateful decisions today when we live in an age where government serves as an authority for everything, constraining even your thought and action in a thousand different ways that functionally make the First Amendment an appendage. Truth has become secondary to happy feelings and the niceties of political correctness, but that can only happen when government has such authority that it exists functionally unopposed as a social actor. Our position today is a result of the direction in which FDR's policies irrevocably launched our country.

The second point he well understood is that politicians are paid to act. There is something in human psychology where we cannot help but value those who appear to act so much more than those who counsel patience. In a time of crisis, we instinctively look for the hero who will rush into the moment and bring salvation. We want big actions, big gestures, and the projection of strength to overcome the weakness each of us feels somewhere deep inside.

The merits of policies arising from crisis, though presented in rhetoric for the few dissidents who question the moment of crisis, are highly suspect. Usually, it is in these times we see rapid expansion of government as the solution to problems, whose origins, often trace back to other government policies. The state grows larger and larger as it attempts to become the answer to all our ills, fulfilling the idea Marx and others pushed where only the state can perfect man from his material misery to some form of freedom. But our day by day practical experience shows this grandeur never really comes down to the little folk.

At least FDR created jobs and his full-throated socialism accomplished far more than say Obama did with his promise of shovel-ready jobs for the new green economy. Back then, even the left was more rooted in reality and more efficient technologies like hydro power, and they gained the benefits of having been seen to care to and to act. Four terms in the Oval Office, an accomplishment of both prowess and vanity, gave the Democrats the start of a 20-year period during which they remade America.

After a whole generation grew up comfortable with the idea government had many roles to play in our lives, the idea that we would return to the freedom we had before the New Deal began to fade. Of course, the government was constrained by the ideas of the times, so we didn't see the push for such divisive ideas as we do today, but it's important to understand their restraint as motivated by a desire to maintain power rather than respect for freedom. The state has its own mandate to expand and maintain control and has ever been assisted by those who are most skillful and least scrupulous to accomplish these ends.

The happy face came first with policies like the TVA which created jobs and brought wealth to an impoverished area in Tennessee, but at the cost of destroying traditional life. The jobs were readily visible and quantifiable, whereas the social destruction was delayed and less obvious. As long as the people in Appalachia were partners in the great mission to expand government to realize greater justice for mankind, for man as matter, they were welcome allies. From FDR to Al Gore, this remained the case, but it's funny how rural folks who had been portrayed so sympathetically before would in a generation's time transform into backward hicks when it was decided their values no longer facilitated this unceasing motion toward government authority.

The point here is that when the left helps people, they do so motivated by a sort of limited regard lacking in human empathy where they see others as having only a certain material need. They take care of the issues like a problem, motivated not by love and spirit or a greater sense of nationalism, but their own form of international humanism that has the warmth of a math equation. Most of their practitioners have the good sense to employ better rhetoric, but when you look at the end game, isn't it always a form, a check, and a list of rules about how life must be lived? In the end, doesn't it always seem to be about taking control?

Stray from that list but a little, or assert your belief in any other higher power, and watch how quickly the state and its myriad allies, assemblages, and controllers will turn on you. The state was made to help the poor rural white folk. And yet now, it oppresses them with great vigor because of their noncompliance, begging the question of whether their involvement was ever about helping people. Was it about honoring our Christian legacy of love and charity, or was it about controlling choices to dictate outcomes?

One could argue this is an unintended side effect of good intentions, but what I would ask then is how many times will we keep giving power away? We hope to see things get fixed by trusting politics to help us, by thinking we can meet some material need that brings utopia, forgetting the basic truth that all we have ever enjoyed is our existence as people, messy and beyond the help of any single idea. Each time we take this chance, we end up with fewer resources, more division, and more oppression.

Furthermore, whenever we give away such authority, the state tries and struggles for a time to make things work. A few successes are speckled by many failures. The state employs every means to defend itself against the indignation of the citizenry, looking to exempt itself from consequence.

A favorite trick is to stack the Courts. FDR initiated that tactic also, looking to expand the Supreme Court to 15 Justices to ease away the impediment of existing law. Though he failed in that regard, liberals never gave up that mission and what the people would never pass on their own, became reality through the intervention of the un-elected. Look how the Courts have consistently been used to work against the sanctity of life, our traditional and protected expression of morality, and until very recently, against our ultimate right to self-defense. Instead of kings, we now have judges set up above us, working in concert with academics who seek to correct our wrong thinking.

But when such actions fail, and public anger threatens to boil over, the state usually has one trick left to play. Knowing our psychology and counting upon our penchant to rally around the flag, how often have we seen war arise at just the right time? The ultimate endeavor in statecraft, war resets the books and forces production forward, revealing the more potent truth that the success of a people is motivated more by their beliefs than any institution or policy. But when the nation gets harnessed to the state for its own self-defense, then in this effort toward self-preservation, the ineffective or oppressive policies the people would otherwise have demanded to be withdrawn are also protected, preserved, and enshrined.

It is customary to present World War II as a great conflict of good versus evil like some Hollywood movie, but once those who spilled blood have passed away, it is almost assured history will drop such facile analysis and instead see something far more complex. World War II was in fact the second act of a Civil War in the western world, catalyzed by economic needs, but also fomented by actors at the periphery of our societies who used these conflicts to gain the means by which they could take control and reshape the west.

The success of their efforts is plain to see today in how the state FDR built upon has expanded far beyond even his wildest imagination, and which has served to constrain our habits and our beliefs in ways which would make the most repressed police-state proud. It's like we emerged from the room and now we truly have learned to love Big Brother…and so now we can expire.

Chapter 6: The Mythology of World War II: A Modern-Day Fairy Tale

World War II is an incredibly complicated subject about which many books have been and continue to be written. Condensing the reasons for what happened and the outcomes which followed into a single chapter inherently involves leaving aside many other ways to consider this scenario. In the interests of time and this narrative, however, it's worth focusing on the ways America was drawn into the war, the consequences of the war for our broader civilization, and how the state transformed and further developed over the course of these battles.

Many people have strong opinions about the larger context of the war, and these questions are of vital significance. Why Europe first and then the rest of the world in succession should be plunged into global conflict just a generation after the supposed war to end all wars needs to be asked. Not just the First World War, but the Spanish Flu decimated the population of many European countries, and then the continent got drawn into a blood-soaked struggle for ideology. Radicalization happened on a massive scale as existing regimes proved either too corrupt or inept to maintain public support.

The Soviet Union went hard left under a totalitarian regime in full blossom under Stalin. Italy and Germany went right, beating back their own socialist and communist threats to elect new forms of nationalism that were as committed to conflict as the left. Britain and France sought to maintain their Empires, and imperial aspirations arose in Japan to equal those. In many ways, the old wars of imperialism and resource collection were infused with a new energy in seeking a truer way to mobilize and unite a given people under a larger goal.

Where did America sit in this equation? As always, we remained a land apart, wanting to enjoy the tranquility our separated continent allowed, and seeking peace and prosperity apart from the interminable conflicts of the ancestral homelands. The people had volunteered for one war already, and not only were the promised Fourteen Points for peace ignored, the League of Nations had proven itself ineffective and the only regard the men who had served in Europe received were to be scattered during the Bonus Army March for daring to request their promised benefits

But FDR and his cohorts understood well that war represented an opportunity to grow the state further, and so he began the process of making America a party to this conflict. For socialism to take root in such foreign soil as America, the idea first had to be planted of an imminent threat sufficient to destroy our very being. In much the same way as the Soviet Union would eventually come to see its whole justification in the Great Patriotic War (their name for WWII) as being to stop Nazism, America accepted this same sort of branding where the nationalist right was presented as an eternal bogeyman, so that in response we needed to become an arsenal of democracy, fighting for all people under this system – increasingly Marxist, socialist, and involuntary by nature.

Over the last seventy years, we have been taught this war was inevitable and it was necessary to defeat a great evil in the Germans specifically. The blood of our many men which was honorably given to accomplish this cause sealed this pact beyond dispute for generations, but such classification requires us to overlook several relevant and very inconvenient facts.

In 1939, when Germany invaded Poland they were not alone in their action. In fact, Germany was merely seeking to reclaim lands they had held for the previous century and then some, prompted by real fears that Germans in that region were being slain by Poles. And in this invasion, prompted as much by British guarantees which they had no functional ability to enforce, the Soviet Union was just as guilty for consuming their own large piece of Poland. We never decry how the Communists just took Poland before they were even our allies, not to mention the many annexations they made afterward.

Furthermore, during 1940 when Germany conquered France, both before and after those strikes, there were many opportunities where all sides could have settled peace with relatively minor adjustments, with Alsace-Lorraine going to

Germany, and without engaging in conflict at a global and genocidal scale. Germany certainly was aggressive, but England was no less intransigent in their willingness to fight. War is complicated, and this idea there was an absolute good guy and bad guy is a dangerous over-simplification.

Just like World War I, as Churchill confirmed in his own history, the hope of the West was in dragging America into the war. In Roosevelt, he had an ally committed to this cause, using Lend-Lease to accomplish the dual goal of forcibly kick-starting the moribund American economy his New Deal policies had failed to stimulate, as well as giving government control over the means of production and for the first time to fully mobilize and unite the American people not around their nation, but instead around their government.

With supplies being sent not just to our traditional allies like England, but also to the Soviet state, the question of this war being a battle for democracy, liberty, and self-determination is thrown wide open. It was understood Stalin had already purged millions of people in 1938, not to mention the state-induced famines like the Holodomor by which the Ukraine was devastated. But the Georgian dictator was re-branded by a complicit media, as leftist and Marxist then as it is now, as friendly Uncle Joe whom we had to supply to keep up the good fight.

It would be the new American trend from World War II forward to support dictators as the lesser of two evils as a means to assert greater power. The argument made then, as now, is that we support totalitarians abroad to ensure our security at home. But has the world or the United States become safer? Or has our intervention all these times only entangled us in a world of conflicts ancient and novel from which we cannot escape, and which distract our attention from regaining choice to select our own manifest destiny?

FDR campaigned on keeping America out of the War, as Wilson had, while doing everything he could to bring America into the war. The Germans didn't bite, seeing the communists in the Soviet Union with the clear ideological vision as the one enemy that must be destroyed. But the Japanese were pushed into engaging the United States by virtue of a crippling embargo, a form of economic warfare, that FDR undertook to push America further into the conflict. FDR succeeded. Japan, desperate as an island nation to break the blockade on fuel, attacked Pearl Harbor in response.

For those more conspiratorially inclined, it's interesting that the most valuable assets of the American fleet, the aircraft carriers, were all safely away from Oahu. For all the code breaking prowess of the United States, and their own war planning conducted by General Mitchell, they had thought Japan might one day try a first strike attack, but security was strangely lax. Rumors persist to this day that the British knew the attack was coming, but the prize of seeing the sleeping giant that was American mobilization brought into the war outweighed integrity, so they failed to warn us.

This is where respectable academics would say this account is crazy, but why? We already know from existing historical records that Britain allowed attacks to happen on their homeland rather than reveal they had broken the German Enigma cipher. States have a different morality than people, and to ensure their survival, they will contemplate many things normal people would consider immoral. Allowing an ally to be attacked and then rushing to offer support and point the war in the right direction is one of the most powerful tools available to states. We've seen how this has been exploited in our lifetimes with Iraq II, and it's reasonable to question whether the same thing happened with Pearl Harbor, especially as the most valuable assets just happened to be out of town.

In any case, the war had begun, and America entered the conflict in 1941 emerging victorious some four years later after hundreds of thousands of lives were lost. We entered the war a republic, but left it an empire, controlling Japan, having hegemony over western Europe, and being asked to assume the status of global hegemon, set in opposition to the alternate view of the other great victor, the Soviet Union.

The war to free Poland ended up with all of Poland and half of Germany besides under Russian control. The

Russians pillaged and raped their way westward, forcibly impregnating millions of women, and entire cities like Konigsberg were depopulated and pushed westward. This is a conveniently untold story in the West, but if you were to examine a map made before 1939, you'd see just how many people were surrendered to the Soviets to expand Russia.

Seeing how the end-result of a war we claim to have won put untold millions of people and entire nations under brutal totalitarian Soviet rule, the import of the whole war comes into question. However, these questions are not to be publicly debated, and so the war in common understanding has become something more akin to a grand alliance to defeat that most evil of dictators whose extreme atrocity was the Holocaust, an event where we are told six million plus Jews as well as others were killed by the Germans.

An entire industry has sprung up around memorializing the Holocaust, using the events which purportedly happened during WWII, putting museums in countries around the world and using the entire mass media to make questioning these figures or anything related to Jewry the greatest of all crimes. Generations removed from these events, the movement is even stronger today than ever before, making it a thought crime to question the motives of any Jewish actor or ask why so many Jews support certain Marxist causes.

Flanked by organizations like the Anti-Defamation League (ADL), organized Jewish interests created a war myth of a grandiose battle of good versus evil that deftly justified the many deaths of Americans in combat for this greater cause while also placing Jews first and later Israelis as a special class immune to the same critique to which all other peoples and states are subject. To even question why Israelis treat Palestinians in much the same way they claim Germans treated them, is to be called another Hitler.

To those willing to reconsider the Second World War with a less prejudiced eye, it's interesting how we are strangely mute about the tens of millions more people slaughtered by the Soviets, not to mention how we never talk about Stalin or Mao, who arose later in China, with the same urgency as the Holocaust It's as if academia has this deep bias of being unable to criticize the left, who killed even more vigorously by standard reckoning, than the Axis managed. But there are those who say both sides were evil, and mirror reflections of one another, which could be fair.

All of that said, some facts about this case have bothered me for some time as a serious historian. Remembering our first insight that narrative matters more than facts, and the key to establishing a narrative is ignoring facts which don't fit, the World Almanac has a strange discontinuity. In 1933, they estimated the Jewish population of Europe to be approximately 9.5 million. In 1948, without any public outcry or push-back, they estimated the number had dipped to just shy of 9.3 million.

Where did the six million people go? It seems improbable that a well-regarded institution like the World Almanac would simply overlook the deaths of so many, which makes one wonder what really happened? I don't have these answers, but what is undeniable is the agenda which was put around these events has made it impossible to publicly discuss what happened until very recently. And even then, people take great risk just to ask for confirmation and honest discussion.

It might seem funny that events from so long ago are still so potent today, but there's a reason for that. If World War II wasn't about the Holocaust, then people might ask other questions, such as why Americans sacrificed their lives to subject millions of Europeans to totalitarian rule. They might also ask why Marxists were given control over so many of the universities and media. Nobody could criticize these Marxists, because being disproportionately Jewish, any criticism, no matter how legitimate, became a matter of anti-Semitic racism. So instead, the majority was trained to remain silent because for the first time in western history, race became how political correctness would be enforced.

Facts became racist. Saying blacks are more likely to commit violent crimes, though demonstrably true by statistics, is racist. Saying Jews are disproportionately able to secure professorships or have massive over-representation in the media, thought easily provable, is racist. Saying Muslims are more likely to commit mass acts of terror than organized groups in the west, though evident, is racist. And the single biggest crime, for which we bled and fought in World War II, was to prevent race from ever being used to look at people.

Except for ourselves. And that's the interesting rub. Before World War II, you would never have heard of white identity as a negative thing. Whether people were proud of their identity or whether they viewed it as a nonentity, we were never fit into some grand narrative as being the root of all evil. That only began when the Cultural Marxists, emerging largely from academics in Frankfurt after the war, decided to paint whites as evil because in each of us, they believed, is another comic book villain like the dastardly Hitler just waiting to come out.

Time will bear out the truth of what the Germans did and did not do. Though the topic is fascinating and worthy of more examination for the reader so inclined, my focus is on how World War II affects us today. The state grew, Marxists everywhere were strengthened, and the attack upon white and western identity were now ready to become a major thing.

For these reasons, World War II may eventually be understood as the culmination of a great civil war within the west, where Marxism won, and the forces of dialectical materialism – which is to say that having stuff would lead to the greatest happiness – defeated the nationalists – those who believed people mattered as the groups they had existed as for many years, and the dissolution of the white race was embraced unanimously as the prize of the victors.

The Soviet Union had always pushed for socialism across all borders, so this fit them perfectly. But what is more interesting is how for all our democratic and capitalist rhetoric, how acquiescent America was in this idea that government would run lives and care for people, and in stepping beyond concern for the people of its own nation, to some form of globalism where the only goal was to take care of all the citizens of the world. It would take decades for these beliefs to crystallize, but with a national security state now fully operable, it was only a matter of will and dedication.

We won the war, but what did it really cost us?

Chapter 7: When Spies Start Looking at You

Throughout history, the tradition has always been that after the final victory of a great war, the men would demobilize and go home. Peace would reign, usually for a generation or more, as those who had already fought had little desire to repeat the same horror. Exceptions naturally abound, but the idea of a time of peace and prosperity following victory is something embedded deep within our psyche as a natural human desire that could only be superseded by some exigent threat.

Remember how the ideas of Hegel were introduced earlier through Marx, of the dialectic where history is presented as the constant tension between two different visions seeking some grand synthesis. Remember also how the Marxists were aided in their desire to take control in the East, in not just Russia but throughout east Asia. As the post-war period arose, they were presented as an equal or greater threat to dominion by the defeated Axis Powers. Against this backdrop, Americans were told that victory over one danger would only be the prelude to a conflict against an Iron Curtain that would now serve to test our mettle.

Without trivializing the very real aspirations of the Communist leadership under Stalin and the massive and patently illegal land grabs they made throughout Eastern Europe, the relevant aspect for America's future is that we would not be permitted to stand down and go home. Instead, the military would remain a colossus, joined now by the beginnings of what would become an omnipresent security state designed to do the things we the people were not to know about for our own protection.

Internally, the Central Intelligence Agency was founded in 1947 with passage of the National Security Act. This act removed the responsibility for intelligence from the military with the traditional Office of Strategic Services, and created a new entity whose stated purpose was to centralize intelligence, avoid law enforcement, and to gain information around the world. It should be obvious that having such power amassed in a central, non-elected entity, especially without the vows of service and duty which uniquely distinguish the military, offered at least the chance for corruption and to hopelessly drag America further into other foreign conflicts.

But the Agency, or the Company as it is sometimes called, is only the logical progression of a series of decisions made to force America to more deeply engage with the world. Many of the globalist institutions that exist today were either directly established, or their suggestive predecessors emerged during that period. The IMF, World Bank, and United Nations are three of the most powerful.

Bretton Woods established the United States Dollar as the world reserve currency, setting us up for the many actions we later took to preserve this status by fighting abroad, though that was never explained clearly to a public which isn't familiar with fiat currency and the arbitrariness of its essential value. America gained prestige and hegemonic status, but at the cost of having to serve as world's policemen, a fact provable by how frequently we go to war and how many places American servicemen are stationed abroad, and which meant the price was never going back to the modest republic envisioned at our founding.

However, having the world reserve currency and being the greatest source of wealth meant we were expected to offer our wealth to fix the world. The Marshall Plan invested many billions in foreign aid from the increasingly heavily taxed population of these United States in what would be the first of many public and not so public actions wherein the wealth of our people was used to keep other parts of the world going. Although individual actions to rebuild may have been good investments, what is inarguable is that the American people were put on the hook to serve as the lender of last resort, a function which they would be called upon repeatedly to fulfill.

Even more than money, the new United Nations was supposed to learn from the failures of the League of Nations and have teeth to intervene to maintain peace. It's no accident Orwell wrote so vividly in this time, because we literally created armies of peacekeepers in discordant powder blue helmets to somehow pretend our wars were something more noble. Perhaps this interpretation is too cynical for those who would hope international peace could be arranged through dialogue but seeing the many UN interventions as examples of incompetence, overreach or corruption, it's hard to argue America has received sufficient value for putting our men and women at their call as we have done so often.

We were told we needed to fight the communists, but we gave the Soviet Union an equal seat at the UN Security Council table, with a veto power that rendered the idea of this grand ideological war moot. Take that as further evidence the conflict between the Russians and Americans was less urgent than suggested. Instead, we undertook a series of proxy wars where we intervened on one side, in places where Americans had never cared previously, and our public was told we needed to engage to protect our grand values of democracy and liberty – by surrendering our own liberty to the war effort.

We entangled ourselves in many new alliances. NATO made us guarantors of Europe. SEATO did the same in Asia. ANZUS brought us into the south Pacific. And we had numerous engagements in Latin America. We were drawn in a thousand different directions, acting in fear and anxiety, but also making real sacrifices without asking what we were doing to the character of our own state.

Those who lived through this time could argue after the carnage of the Second World War, it was justified to do anything that was necessary to prevent another conflict so devastating. Doubting their sincerity from this distance would be unfair, but let's look what they gave up. They gave spying powers to the government. They created the alphabet soup of agencies which today represent the eponymous Deep State that exists above and beyond the officials we elect as a permanent and largely hidden bureaucracy. Taxation had risen many times over in just two generations, and with that newfound wealth and authority, government began looking for new programs and ideas by which it could reshape America.

It is a truism in government that once an agency receives a certain amount of budget, they will find ways to spend the entire amount whether need warrants such investment or not because it's much harder to get new money appropriated than justify the previous year's expenditure. I know this firsthand from working for years as purchasing director for a government contractor, seeing a microcosm of how the whole American economy in many sectors and for many people would ebb and flow in response to government contracts and spending. Eisenhower would term this the military industrial complex at the end of the next decade, but these were its formative years and all those parties interested in shaping the future learned quickly the magic words to get government money.

As always and as ever, either the threat of war or the actual reality of such was the means through which the

American colossus kept rolling. With all these new responsibilities and expenditures, we couldn't be allowed the natural retraction to a less vigorous economy, so instead we started actively seeking a way to find happiness through perpetual growth. If you imagine that would create insane bubbles, then we share the same opinion and there are a few episodes worth detailing as we advance, including always and foremost the numerous times we've had to inflate and therefore debase our own currency. But, for now, let's focus on the first war of peace: Korea.

Writing in 2018, the Korean War still has not been resolved. A truce was reached in 1953 for a war started by an invasion in 1950, but it is still unresolved some 65 years later. The details of the communists in the North invading South are well known. The United Nations approved intervention, thanks to trickery to avoid a certain veto by the Soviets who would have supported the North even as they remained in the UN. The defeat of the North was prevented by the intervention of the Chinese, leading to massive loss of life on all sides, and the resolution of the war was not victory, but stalemate as the political leadership chose such action rather than intensifying the war. Many died, nothing was solved, but lots of money was spent: The new model.

While those who live in South Korea enjoy a much better standard of life than their Northern counterparts, one is tempted to ask why America was involved in this mess. Intelligent justifications like containment, the Truman

Doctrine of encircling the Soviet sphere of influence found credit in academic journals and among geopolitical strategists. Domino theory would evolve from this with the argument that once communism took root anywhere, it would take root everywhere. The ideological death match between communism and capitalism would be fought out on a hundred different national chess boards, but the question remains: Was if it was worth our action?

War without victory and the management of peace became a familiar refrain. Our men would fight, die, and bleed, and we would make nice with our alleged enemies a generation later. Military intervention became more popular, and in time, the War Powers act evolved to allow our President to have wars without declarations. Few know this, but the United States hasn't legally declared war on any country since 1942, but we have had multiple conflicts in many other places because our country has shifted from the control of the people through their elected representatives, and instead now we have a security state.

We built up the apparatus of the security state to fight the Soviet Union. We created our own secret police to do so, structured our entire economy in so many ways to serve this purpose, and fought wars and supported tyrants for the greater good. It's amazing how much like socialism that sounds, but that is the Marxist trick. These fights we enter make us like our enemies, and in so doing, make us very much the same as one another. While they had a command economy, and we had a market economy, both were materialist philosophies obsessed with their own version of truth and willing to impose it at any cost. No wonder the Cold Warriors understood each other so well.

Therefore, more than a quarter century removed from the Cold War, the fifties took on a different light. In many ways, that relatively peaceful decade was the last chance to disassemble the emerging colossus of the state, and offers guidance for today about what communism is, how it took control, and understanding that its form was not just Russian, but all too often American in character.

Chapter 8: The Last Stand of Traditional America

With the fervor being spread about the threat posed by the Soviet Union, it was only natural that Americans would begin looking for traitors within, for communists in our ranks whose loyalty to that corrupt ideology outranked their commitment to the nation. There was fertile ground for such a search, and beneath the tranquil exterior of the 1950's, the fight to find these double agents marked much of the decade.

Probably the best-known figure of these times was Senator Joseph McCarthy of Wisconsin who helped coordinate efforts to identify saboteurs and persons of interest. For years, his efforts helped uncover many people, prominent in academia, media, and often of foreign descent who sold or gave our national secrets to the Soviet Union. With figures like Julius and Ethel Rosenberg uncovered by his and other related efforts, there was real progress in unraveling a network that existed not just to help Russia, but rather existing above and beyond both nations as a group of people motivated by Marxism to fundamentally change humanity.

For his efforts, he was rewarded with unceasing ridicule by a hostile press, which in those days could still exist with some facade of impartial neutrality. His patriotic diligence culminated in an infamous accusation that called his decency into question, destroying his investigation, and turning this good man into a symbol of national derision and made to look a fool for his supposed paranoia.

Instead of using my characterization of what the Senator sought to find, allow me to share his own words from a speech he gave in 1950 describing the threat America faced. Consider carefully, with the benefit of several generations for the agenda to play out, if his words were correct or if he was delusional. The speech he gave in Wheeling, West Virginia on February 9th, 1950 is worth reading in full, but this excerpt is perhaps most relevant to today:

"This indicates the swiftness of the tempo of Communist victories and American defeats in the cold war. As one of our outstanding historical figures once said, "When a great democracy is destroyed, it will not be from enemies from without, but rather because of enemies from within...

The reason why we find ourselves in a position of impotency is not because our only powerful potential enemy has sent men to invade our shore... but rather because of the traitorous actions of those who have been treated so well by this Nation. It has not been the less fortunate, or members of minority groups who have been traitorous to this Nation, but rather those who have had all the benefits that the wealthiest Nation on earth has had to offer... the finest homes, the finest college education and the finest jobs in government we can give.

This is glaringly true in the State Department. There the bright young men who are born with silver spoons in their mouths are the ones who have been most traitorous..."

Given a fair fight, the American people have never lost a war. But given that same fairness, we have allowed ourselves for many generations to be open to new ideas and new people giving them the same courtesy which many of us received upon our arrival. We are optimists who expect the best of people, and who hope for our most talented and gifted people to serve the national interest.

But what ideas do those people learn when they matriculate in our elite institutions? Swarthmore, the college I attended which annually ranks among the best in the nation, was lovingly known as the Kremlin on the Crum. When I was a student there in the 1990's, I remember professors who wore black each day lamenting the fall of the Soviet Union. While they certainly did not have control of colleges in the 1950's to the extent they do today, it's no secret academia has been a beacon for those who teach hatred in many ways of western, white, and American thought, all three being seen as evil forms of exploitation.

In fact, just as with the media, academia continues pushing a Marxist ideology which ultimately is rooted in the idea of theft – of forceful redistribution to remedy the supposed failings of nature and create a more just society. It is natural for people to resist involuntary expropriation, so the kindly rhetoric of "from each according to his ability to each according to his need" inevitably becomes violent and seeks to grow the compulsory power of the state to force people to embrace this generous and self-righteous ethic.

Consider the views of bureaucrats within government, and how they almost uniformly lean hard left, working to forever constrain the liberties of the people to realize the elusive justice they seek. Bureaucrats believe they could create a utopia and realize their dream of equality … if only given yet more control. Though their victory has not yet been complete here in America, they do succeed from time to time in imposing their ideas, and they often reach their stated goal of equality, as can be seen in Detroit.

The experiment invariably ends in abject poverty and the state breaking down because it is unable to fulfill the basic needs of its own people. Citizens stop working except for what the black market manages, and the war of all against all becomes realized as people seek only to survive. Marxism breaks down civilization, as it has most recently done in Venezuela where an oil-rich country now cannot provide toilet paper and rumors escape of cannibalism and desperate citizens eating zoo animals to survive. It was no different for China in the 1950's when the Great Leap Forward and Cultural Revolution saw mass death and delirium in the misguided idea that history can be made to fit an idea.

Yet, these ideas remain not only present, but predominant among academia, media, and government today, and we are forced to ask from whence they came. Marxist ideas clearly date back well before 1910 but gained traction due to the growth of government through income taxes to support such insanity and the private Federal Reserve bank for financing. Marxism and communism were most certainly active during the time of McCarthy.

It is now known that those same foreign scientists treated like gold in America sent Stalin the secrets from the Manhattan Project and later research on more powerful nuclear weapons. Why they would betray their adoptive home country is an interesting question that forces us to ask once more where their loyalty lay. For the Marxist, it seems he is always a globalist, driven by ideas and an identity that exists in his mind above and beyond whatever land he inhabits.

Perhaps that is why so many Jews end up Marxists, because their own diaspora had similar traits, where they existed apart and beyond the host culture, and worked instead on ideas instead of with people. We demonstrated how heavily involved they were with the creation of the Soviet Union above the Russian people, and here again we find disproportionate involvement in the names which were considered collaborators with the Communists. Is it not just as likely they were helping their own people as any desire to help the Russians?

Now, talking about Jews today will get you in more trouble than McCarthy got into for talking about the red threat in his day, but it's a conversation we desperately need to have and not in some facile form where we simply state all Jews are evil or, by contrast, the currently accepted dogma where Jews are beyond criticism. They are undoubtedly a bright and talented people who succeed greatly within the west and whose accomplishments are manifold, but we should ask: why we keep finding them far more than any natural distribution whenever efforts are made to undo our society?

Seeking knowledge of the motives of any people is not a negative effort. I seek to understand why America lost its moral center, how we shifted from a country that emphasized achievement and continuity to one that is frankly, in many ways, a lesser version of itself where people cry victimhood and we see the ongoing effort to replace both our traditional people and ideas. In looking into how it has happened, which this account shares in brief, it becomes clear we did it to ourselves through the ideas McCarthy sought to prevent. But we also see the same group constantly pushing this secular, materialist, and amoral path forward.

I do not blame individuals for what they think, as I know many people exist within Jewry and every other group who are just as aware and troubled by what their compatriots have done. In truth, they're some of the biggest supporters of my effort to bring these arguments into the light, because these discussions happen daily in places where the media isn't welcome. These conversations are necessary because enforced silence increases the likelihood of violence on terms very similar to that of the past. Working against that in a sincere way – unlike censors who think they can somehow control secrets in a digital age – is thankless, but necessary, because the argument against McCarthy was wrong.

The idea that decency should override truth is at the heart of the American crisis. We don't say things that are offensive because we don't want people to feel bad, but in so doing, we have enabled people to build a future based upon fictions rather than facts. That is the Marxist trick where we create cultural policy based upon what we wish were true, and then when people don't behave as predicted by the flawed model, the effort fails and civilization decays. There is always room for aspiration to improve and be better versions of ourselves, but we can only get there when we root ourselves in factual reality and practice and be frank about what we do well and what we don't.

But that's not what happens today. Today, we blame whites, men, Christians, conservatives, and western ideas for all the ills of society. Leaving aside the small inconvenient fact these groups were responsible for most of the many best attributes of America specifically and the West generally, we have been appropriated as legitimate targets for ridicule, and as the only groups who can be talked about in a negative fashion in America without being "prejudicial", we are blamed for everything.

They're right in one regard. We built western civilization. We were kind enough, unlike any other group in history, to allows others into our midst, because we had faith enough in our ideas and the goodness of humanity to try this experiment. It seems to be failing in most places, honestly, as our culture gives way and we find materialism alone isn't enough to sate the acquisitiveness it spawns, whether in our own greedy hearts or in those refugees we welcome to our shores who consume just as voraciously.

But that came later, and in the quiet of the 1950's, we saw brave efforts to tackle the Marxist idea fail at the altar of political correctness. We got an entrenched military industrial complex to fight the Soviet threat on the battlefield, ensuring money flowed through industry and finance, and then back again to the government. But the very core idea of communism, this Marxist ideal, would never be seriously challenged again as it ate into the heart of our being.

The people who might have led this resistance, the John Birch Society were derided as cranks, and instead Bill Buckley was promoted straight from Yale, from whence so many future pre-selected leaders would come, and he would define an acceptable form of conservatism: Banter and acquiescence. High minded idealism was permissible, but calling out the enemy within was plebeian, thus paving the way for the left to take greater control.

That said, there was potentially one last effort to fight off the military industrial complex, in the name of Americans who did not want perpetual war, and it came from a young and idealistic President who seemed to realize just what problems had come into being when he was elected in 1960. His assassination was a trauma which would forever change politics. Let's look at yet another reason why Kennedy was murdered.

Chapter 9: Everyone Hates Kennedy

Perhaps no event in American History has spawned more controversy and conspiracy theories than the assassination of President John F. Kennedy in Dallas, Texas on November 22, 1963. Reams of literature have been written about the event, with those who lived through those times remembering it as a moment of great sadness where the optimism and hope of this nation was forever lost. Camelot, as his administration was known, had fallen, but questions remain regarding who toppled the castle.

An official inquiry known as the Warren Commission concluded that Lee Harvey Oswald was the single shooter, a nut case who had interesting and confusing ties among many different groups including some Cuban dissidents. With crack shots from the Book Depository and trajectories for the bullets fired from his Carcano rifle professional marksmen doubt are even possible, he was assigned full responsibility for the crime. It would have been interesting to hear Oswald's defense, but he was murdered just two days later by Jack Ruby, a man born as Jacob Rubenstein in Chicago, and who ran a night club in Texas. Those are the facts we know.

Many people express great skepticism about the results of the politically assembled Warren Commission. With the national tragedy seemingly redeemed by the execution of the killer, a nation's anger and grief were sufficiently sated for conclusions to be drawn that prevented more critical inquiry. The Dallas Police, who then treated the assassination as a local crime rather than the Federal crime it has since become, and the District Attorney were content to accept the given conclusion. But assuming you are a little more skeptical, there are no shortage of people who could have individually or collectively played a role in what happened on that day.

Before examining each of them, a funny story. On that same fateful day, not only was Vice-President Lyndon B. Johnson, a stalwart from the US Senate representing Texas who was attached to Kennedy against some opposition at the Democratic National Convention in Dallas, but so was Richard Nixon who would succeed him. Even more interesting, though he would later deny being in Dallas and have no special recollection of the day, documents surfaced about a certain George Bush being there that day as an agent. More key names like FBI Director J. Edgar Hoover had been there just the day before, which is strange because you wouldn't usually see so many people gathered in a place that was just supposed to be a Presidential visit.

Who would benefit from Kennedy's death? The list is not short, and both he and his brother Robert F. Kennedy who would be assassinated just a few years later during his own abortive campaign for President against LBJ in the 1968 Democratic Primary by Sirhan Sirhan, had made no shortage of enemies.

Examination should start with LBJ. Forced onto the ticket by the power-brokers of the Democrat Party, LBJ had been a titan of the Senate and was known to be a bully. Stories of his corruption were legendary, and it has long been alleged LIFE Magazine, with information fed by RFK, was prepared to print an article detailing how deep this corruption ran in the November 27th issue from 1963 which would have gone to print on the 24th. Much of the information centered around Bobby Baker, a page who had served LBJ during his time in the Senate and had made millions running an informal racket called the Quorum Club. The details of this racket are fascinating, as well as the even more troubling stories from his time in Texas that suggest LBJ had long had the police there in his back pocket.

It was no secret that Kennedy did not like Johnson and did not want him on the ticket. It's an unfortunate recurring theme in which Presidents who have at least somewhat outsider tendencies are saddled with running mates connected deeply within the Establishment. A perfect example from the Republican side is how Bush was added to the Reagan ticket. Whether that is considered balance or insurance is an interesting question, but what seems true is the money men, which includes the Deep State bureaucracies that live off military contracts as well as other actors, have a vested interest in who sits at 1600 Pennsylvania Avenue.

LBJ had two compelling reasons to act. He needed to preserve his own future rather than being taken down by political scandal, and any political aspirations he had required Kennedy to be removed and his own issues to disappear. While he could not have done this alone, Kennedy had made many enemies in other parts of the government who could have helped.

Organized crime was not happy with the results they had helped deliver in 1960. Kennedy infamously defeated Nixon with votes coming in from Chicago which had been delivered by the Daly machine. The Democratic Party had long been running the Second City as a sinecure, and in exchange for the votes they would deliver, there was an implicit understanding that the existing arrangement would be honored. Perhaps this accommodation is best described by the incredible comment by J. Edgar Hoover that there was no organized mafia in America.

Robert, who served as Attorney General, violated that agreement by taking a tough stance on crime and trying to faithfully fulfill the duties for which he had been appointed. Several high-profile cases had soured not just the syndicates, but also the bureaucracy which had seemed to reach a level of accommodation required to transact business under Hoover. If it helps, think of today how police sometimes have rings of informants to track higher level crimes, or more cynically, perhaps to insulate those at the top from prosecution. Then, as today, money dominated and so the

Kennedy Brothers had a set of enemies within organized crime and the bureaucracies that cooperated with the syndicates.

Another disaffected group were the Cuban exiles and their CIA Handlers. After the bungled Bay of Pigs Invasion, there were quite a few people who were angry at the betrayal of the effort to remove Castro. This conspiracy gets a lot of attention because Oswald had numerous links to the refugee community in New Orleans, and also because the people involved with this had been involved in a number of bloody fights both on and off their island. In addition to the exiles themselves, the CIA had been embarrassed badly when the President refused to issue additional support for their landing in April of 1961.

Where the Central Intelligence Agency consistently sought to expand American influence with war and instability invariably following, Kennedy actually worked to restrain such tendencies, staring down new Soviet leader Nikita Khrushchev. Instead of looking to delve more deeply into the rising conflict in Vietnam which happened after the French withdrawal from what had previously been known as French Indo-China, he looked to limit our presence. The problem is war was good for business, and the Agency has ever had links to ensure our economy is always running on a wartime footing by creating a degree of instability. Where JFK had moved away from war, LBJ would then accelerate this and the tragedy of Vietnam would begin with the murder of the 35th President.

Kennedy had a real knack for making the right enemies. Although it is not widely known outside of the conspiracy community, he gave a speech decrying the power of the secret society in America in April of 1961 at the same time the Bay of Pigs black ops were undertaken. It is worth listening to this speech, especially in concert with the admonition of Eisenhower's Farewell Address talking about the military industrial complex and how it was taking control of an ever larger, ever more dangerous, and unaccountable portion of government.

There are adherents of other theories, such as the Israelis being upset with JFK for seeking to forestall their rise to nuclear power with the infamous Dimona reactor, Soviet agitators taking retribution against the President for actions throughout the world, and more obscure ideas with figures outside government taking out their grievances. But as we have seen so often throughout this examination, money always plays a role. For all the people he pissed off, perhaps the one that did him in was the banks.

Executive Order 11110, signed June 4, 1963 by President Kennedy, instructed the US Treasury to resume printing of silver certificates to exist as an alternative and potentially as a replacement for the notes issued by the Federal Reserve Bank. Kennedy threatened the monopoly of the Fed. There is literally no institution in America with more purchasing power than the Federal Reserve Bank, which we have already established as a private banking cartel set up under questionable auspices and which exists, even today, largely outside public oversight. The justification for our money being handled by a private cartel is that the economy is too important to be subject to political interference. The reality is those who have money exist above and beyond the law, as they always have to some extent. But we have somehow managed to turn such a state of affairs into both law and a principle of how our state functions.

Taken in sum, we had a criminal Vice-President who had every reason to pull together a coalition of pissed off war financiers, bankers, both law enforcement and the intelligence agencies with mob and dissident allies, all focused against one man trying to do what sounded like good things for our country. Americans love liberty, reduced government, peace, and avoiding unnecessary conflict, but the Deep State dies and withers when the fear disappears, the urgency abates, and people start thinking instead of feeling.

The decades of effort which had reached culmination in the national security stated launched during World War II and retained afterward in the Cold War tension, was not going to simply submit. Instead, it used the skills and talents it had to do what it does best: regime change. Whichever agent was responsible, it seems far more likely they had reason to remove Kennedy than Oswald, a sleeper agent who was likely set up to be a patsy if you read his own complicated story.

In mutual vice, all the characters got what they wanted. LBJ became President, a debacle which sadly warrants its own chapter, and which fundamentally transformed American society. The war was escalated in Vietnam with many thousands of deaths and casualties and billions spent on armaments. The mafia continued business as usual. The Fed became more powerful, and the enforcement arm of Wall Street, the Central Intelligence Agency, gained the power to intervene in even more places around the world. Wherever we find ourselves at war, it's almost a given they were there first.

After JFK passed, many people came to feel the country was lost. In retrospect, those who lived through those tumultuous times often express how that inclination has only grown in strength with the passage of years. In my own judgment, despite having many well-known personal failings and making many mistakes, I've come to think JFK was likely a good man trying to take steps to roll back a state which had escaped control, and who failed. Had he succeeded, it might not have been too late to stop the juggernaut we now face and confront that indubitably exists above us, not as a representation of who we are.

Throughout this profile, much attention has been given over to the people involved and their own aspirations because we sometimes hide intent by couching actions in terms of institutions and not people. There is value in thinking that institutional entities will seek to protect themselves, but to really ascertain what Kennedy had restrained, we need to look critically at what forces Johnson gave free rein over society. Camelot had fallen, and in its place, the Great Society would begin.

Chapter 10: Cultural Marxism: How to Resent Everyone Not Like You

Before delving into the policy details of just what Johnson accomplished as President, a small side trip is necessary to provide context to the ideas behind his policies. For this, we need to look at a movement which was catalyzed in Frankfurt, Germany, but which had found fertile ground across American universities: Cultural Marxism.

Much time has been spent talking about dialectical theory for one simple reason. While it is highly problematic to use this to address history or predict the future, the forces of the left to one extent or another all behave as if these ideas are true. They structure our lives to answer their experiments, and beginning in the 1960's, Marxism evolved in a major way which reflects how it still operates today. Instead of trying to empower individuals from economic poverty, which had been the prior justification given, the new logic was to support groups in their struggle against the centers of power. The politics of liberation and emancipation began to replace those of redistribution, at least in terms of rhetorical flourish.

Put another way, Marxist theory evolved to pit the minority against the majority, seeking to balance power by taking from the status quo authorities. In America, that meant not just the racial majority, but also the traditional culture of work and ownership and the traditional faith of Christianity with natural male and female gender roles. They would seek to destroy society as it was and build something better and fairer by forcing conflict upon the rest of us.

With LBJ, these cultural Marxists found someone willing to adopt their program wholesale. Government would be given authority to make judgments in education, mandate health care decisions, control school curricula, and to undertake the beginning of one of the greatest feats of wealth redistribution in history. American society before Johnson was still largely built upon the idea that one had to work to survive and be a part of America, but under his plans, welfare was massively expanded in every form – so much so that a person could now live completely off Federal subsidy.

As justification for these reforms, historical injustices were cited then as they are now today. Because of what happened 100 years prior, the government needed to take care of vast groups of society, most notably but not exclusively minorities. Cradle to grave support was imagined, and it just so happened that this is when minorities became the most reliable voters for the Democratic Party. In place of opportunity, handouts were offered, and the work ethic needed for true empowerment – with choice – was abandoned in favor of government control.

Johnson succeeded in these actions thanks to public support post Kennedy to heal the wounds, but also an incredibly active Civil Rights movement. Black people were joined by Hispanics, Native Americans, and a great many white people as well to realize the equal protection under law which all people deserve. Such grievances were legitimate then as they are now and would have fit naturally into the desire for a single American culture based on work and opportunity.

But what was offered was more than just equal footing. The Civil Rights Act may have guaranteed equal access to the ballot box, but what people don't realize is it also gerrymandered districts to guarantee certain places had black representation. The rhetoric used in public by respectable faces shown in media was the language of equality, but the letter of the law was different: A different set of laws would now govern the protected minority against a presumptively persecuting majority. Johnson, in endorsing these acts, is widely purported to have shared that he did so because he knew these would change voting habits for a generation. Civil Rights equated to Black Power, as the athletes honestly admitted then as today.

What is the legacy of these reforms today? Consider Section 8 Housing, an idea designed to provide access to better living. Many cities throughout the United States took advantage of the opportunity to provide Federally funded housing, which was supposed to create great opportunity.

Though some people availed themselves of these chances, how many instead decided that getting free or heavily subsidized housing represented new proof that the government would take care of them? Today, a drive through one of these communities in any of the places they can be found throughout our nation is suggestive.

Whereas America in 1900 had more restrictive ballot access, we also had a smaller and less involved government. Adding women, minorities, and younger people, mobilized specifically by government to grow government, unsurprisingly accelerated control away from the individual for their own destiny and into the hands of the state. Without arguing the merit of expanded ballot access here, we observe the reasons these measures are given popular support is directly caught up in the desire to use government to change the social agenda.

Anyone questioning these acts today is pilloried as a racist, but the question we should be asking is why government decided to change who they help? Why did the Democratic Party shift from being at least nominally a party seeking to eradicate poverty as a general concern, as was the rhetoric during FDR, to one that would look to protect certain classes of people? Could it be not because of some trumped up social justice concerns, but instead because of the desire to build a different political coalition to remake the country?

As evidence to this supposition, the Hart-Cellar Act of 1965 is perhaps the most important and most transformational action of the 1960's for us living today, though few speak about it directly and consider the implications. America had historically restricted immigration to only people who came from cultures broadly compatible with our own. But this Act changed the fundamental nature who we brought into our nation. Instead of bringing in people who shared our values of work and the Christian heritage, the new system was designed to encourage immigration from the Third World with quotas and chain migration. What had once been the barest trickle quickly became a flood of new people whose presence would radically transform America.

If the Great Society were truly about ending poverty and helping minorities, as the standard history likes to preach, why would it be coupled with immigration reform which brought in huge numbers of unskilled workers whose primary purpose would be as cheap labor competing largely against the existing poor? Adding new people from Africa, Latin America, and other places would not solve the ongoing problems in existing minority and poor communities, but it would increase the numbers of poor at the exact same time as their radicalization, owing at least in part to government policy once more, would grow.

Culture is a delicate thing. America may be a nation of immigrants, but it also is a country of not just ideology but identity. We held certain moral values that came from our Christian traditions across the various nations of Europe. We agreed to the concept of freedom through work, freedom from interference unlike the rewrite FDR pushed through claiming government existed to give us freedom from consequence. The 1950's saw cultural peace, but with a changing population and radicalization of politics, the simple and great American Dream was assaulted and eventually shattered.

Where we had once enjoyed a single culture and peace and prosperity, we would now be expected to coexist as multiple cultures, with people being rushed into our society from every foreign source possible to correct our injustices. For our supposed sins, we would be asked to redress these by giving more money into government control, to preferential programs, and even reparations directly in some cases. The majority had been the builders of society before, but we were now inverted into being the oppressors, and the academics and politicians teamed up once more to expand the state and seek their egalitarian utopia.

We have this blind spot in America because we're mostly decent people who think ideas run our society. Even though there is a certain limited truth to that idea, the way we come to our ideas is much more complicated than just the reasoned arguments through which we process our public discourse. Yes, the details matter, but we pretend people exist as individuals absent their cultural context and that we are all just blank slates waiting to find the best policy for the greater good. We assume the best of those who want to come here, as an act of faith, but the price has been our cultural stability.

Even if the vast majority of the people who came here had good intentions, which they very likely did, my question is why did the politicians bring them here? It wasn't to help the poor, because they were a net drag on resources. It wasn't to preserve our culture, because they came from places very different than America. Was it altruism? The purveyors of the policies, the same cynical people who had no problem expanding wars in Vietnam and exploiting their own political power, seem unequal to such benefit of the doubt. So instead, isn't it more likely that they were beginning a fundamental transformation of America?

We don't like to say this, but it is indubitably true that if you change the people of a place, you change the nature of that place. Within America, look how successive amnesty bills changed California from a home of Republican governors to a state that is so incredibly progressive that it openly flouts the Federal Government in its quest to favor illegals over citizens. Look to the Europeans whose police forces now protect the foreign migrants over citizens when rapes occur, and violence is threatened. Look to how our states together have taken the power of the citizenry, transferred our wealth to people we welcomed as guests, and then blamed us, the majority, for their failures when they exhaust the handouts we so generously submit.

This was the agenda envisioned by the cultural Marxists, promoted by the universities, enacted by the politicians, and which has in many cases accomplished its main goal. The majority became steadily less wealthy after the 1950's and the minority obtained much more help from the government. The society strove for equality, always at the expense of opportunity, and established precedents wherein justice entailed stealing from those who came earlier to support those chosen to be wards of the state.

It was unfair to the majority then, and it is still unfair today. But it was even worse for the minorities themselves, because while they did receive help from the government, they learned so well to live in dependency that all these programs really accomplished was to perpetually enshrine their poverty. It would take many more years for that to become clear, assisted by other social programming from our bloated Federal state, but the results don't lie. The poor are poorer today, relatively speaking, than they were before these measures were enacted.

As it turns out, having multiple competing cultures in the same space benefits no one. Frustration builds, anger rises, and different modes of being challenge one another. But our government embraced the chaos in many ways, adding the controversy of Vietnam, a war as much by choice as need, to the potent brew of unhappiness it stirred up in the 1960's. As counter-intuitive as it sounds, always keep in mind that government thrives on conflict, because the more problems it creates, the more license the public gives it to act to change things.

For the radicals running the show under LBJ, the Deep State Marxist agenda was just getting started.

Chapter 11: The Domino Theory Only Works Against Us

Order arises out of chaos. The more radical the new order is to be, the more chaotic the scene must become to enable it. This might sound contradictory compared to the way conventional wisdom sees development as linear or at least sequential. But when thinking in terms of human psychology, it begins to make much better sense. Our brains can only process so much at a given time. With space to operate and good information, we tend to make much more reasoned decisions more in keeping with a linear model. But when we feel overwhelmed, our capacity for ordered thought decreases substantially.

At the same time major social transformation was happening in both the size and scope of government as discussed, adding a highly unpopular war into the mix would seem a recipe for disaster. The Vietnam War spawned a huge antiwar movement motivated by many different causes. Drug culture was being thrust into the forefront with music and a sexual/cultural revolution as will be covered in a succeeding chapter. Taken together, suddenly so much was happening so quickly that a person might not even know what to protest or where to fight.

In fact, the breadth, scope and speed of the combination was imposed upon traditional Americans with such overwhelming odds, that it can be understood if a reasoning person might just give up. The overwhelmed American might conclude that everything was corrupt and embrace a sort of all-encompassing nihilism that sought to destroy all that came before. Spurred on by academics and tacitly supported by the media, the energy of confusion spawned by the potent ferment of the 1960's pushed Americans into questioning the value of any action, of reason itself, and all institutions that had previously upheld order.

Relativism is a very unnatural condition for the human mind, believing all things equal to all other things, and it almost has to be grafted by making people both hurt and indifferent at once. It is irrelevant whether such status was deliberately sought or a happy accident for those who wanted to remake society with the state as their ultimate tool, provided the outcome is the same. And for that energy to coalesce, a war without purpose made great sense.

The justification for Vietnam was relatively straightforward in terms of Cold War dialectical logic. Since the Communists had fought to a standstill in Korea, China had assumed hegemony in Asia, and were threatening southeast Asia. Vietnam was a domino that could not be allowed to fall, according to the rough containment strategy that harkened back to Harry Truman. Ho Chi Minh and his North Vietnamese Army were ideologically driven Communists, and in what would be recurring feature of our foreign policy, we backed a corrupt regime to resist them.

As far as the history of Vietnam goes, it was one in a series of a great many countries where decolonization was still ongoing, with the French having been forcibly expelled after World War II. Whereas the imperial powers had formerly kept a sense of order, financial inability and moral unwillingness to maintain their empires, drew them back to their home countries. Old conflicts and rivalries previously suppressed by imperial control flared up again as the empires withdrew, creating highly localized but bloody problems.

Set against the broader backdrop of the Cold War, such feuds were used as wedges by one side or the other to ensure conflict reigned everywhere. Never so hot as to threaten nuclear annihilation, the simmer of war raged throughout Africa, Latin America, and the less developed portions of Asia where resources were funneled by the billions to dictators of all persuasions for just a few cheap words of rhetoric. Our government knew these people were sons of bitches, as they were often called, but so long as they knew which direction to point the guns, we'd support them.

Jack Kennedy recognized clearly that Vietnam was likely to develop into the same sort of quagmire Korea had become where war was fought without intent of victory, a strategic calculation in a balancing game between two sides seeking to gauge one another in blood and treasure. The irony of these fights between two systems so delicately connected is painful, but that symbiosis actually sustained both in productive development, with the fear that comes from uncertainty serving as a motivation to keep citizens engaged.

The genuine rhetoric against the Red Menace within the state as promoted by McCarthy and others was inverted by the government to compel patriotic Americans into taking their concerns into the fight abroad. It is hard to imagine Vietnam ever representing the same sort of threat to America that having traitors in our midst could accomplish, but those who run our state understand all too well how strong the impulse is to rally around the flag.

Wanting to defend one's nation and one's people is among our best and most useful instincts. It's how we preserve our families. But sadly, it is also how the right is most commonly tricked into doing the bidding of the left, agreeing to grow the state for wars which never seems to find resolution. And then those same powers are used to restrain the citizenry at home. An attack against the homeland requires a vigorous response, and all patriots make sacrifices, but the freedom they sacrificed at home never returns.

But men die, of courage, honor, and dignity. Their sacrifices, most given involuntarily, demand respect for bravery and valor, but also there is sadness here. We see time and time again the best men of our generations, and not just in America, sent to foreign shores in these abstruse conflicts, dulling the edge of the knife which could fight here at home to preserve our liberties. We exhaust our energies, both mentally and physically, upon police actions and wars with goals that don't make sense.

LBJ wanted to expand Vietnam, but we were never serious about the winning the war. Winning the peace was inserted as Orwellian double-think, where rules of engagement were designed to never threaten the enemy, even as our men were exposed and put in peril. Instead of an invasion and the full usage of our arsenal to level Hanoi and achieve victory, we wandered through jungles for years. When Goldwater offered potential for a stronger resolution in 1964, he was attacked as a warmonger by those who argued peace required a more limited war. Think how crazy it is that peace required war without victory, yet that is what was sought.

People at home were angry. Men were sent to die in a war without purpose, and that anger boiled over. Too often, those who opposed the conflict took the blame out on the soldiers, dividing the people who fought for the nation from those they were fighting to serve. Far too often this dynamic absolved the government of the blame it deserved for expanding this conflict. For too many, the movement started with the intention of defending the soldiers, but it was instead co-opted into yet another left-wing movement to give government more control.

This is the frustrating and dangerous part of being an activist. Having spent years working as one, both in formal and informal contexts, what you quickly discover is how the movement lovingly cultivated from the grassroots for a noble purpose can be easily compromised by a little money and power, morphing into its complete opposite. I spoke out with love for my race, for white people, and just a few activists and a complicit media would have had you believed I was seeking the destruction of all not like me. They take what is special, what has value, and turn and twist it until all that matters is destroyed. This is how patriotism is used, and the state knows the greatest injury you can inflict upon it is to genuinely care about the plight of your fellow man and to do something about it personally.

The state wants you to not care, because they want you to cede control to them. Marxism requires such a dictatorship of your betters, who take the burden off your hands and take responsibility for as many aspects of life as they are allowed. They will pick the wars because people cannot understand foreign policy. They will select who is to be protected, because they must always balance the unhappy against the restless. They will single out the voice of reason, putting it to their purpose, and then distracting once more.

We could have won Vietnam, probably quite easily had the military been allowed to engage in full mobilization toward victory. But a long war was good for the defense industry, which was churning after the removal of Kennedy. More importantly, it kept people at home on edge, encouraging them to use government in ways never contemplated before and mostly antithetical to the Constitution itself, a clear statement of limited government where individual liberty was the prime restraint against state oppression. Johnson passed the Great Society and we were encouraged to come together at home, seeking unity in a novel synthesis.

By the time Nixon came to power, the Tet Offensive had already happened, and the media parlayed that deception into a grand maneuver designed to begin the long process of extracting America from Vietnam. Having taught our lesson and measured ourselves, those who played the games of statecraft decided no more blood had to be sacrificed at the altar of political expediency.

A war which should not have happened worked slowly toward an end. But the men who went over there and the families who lost loved ones, many of whom never returned and whose ultimate fate remains unknown, were not given the gratification of victory. There was no resolution of point, only the dead and the living. And that is what Marxism offers us in the end, whether it was from the Soviet Communists who were blunter about their agenda, or the socialists within our own country who dish up the same: Material sustenance for a life with no greater meaning.

That people still held sincere belief in patriotism and service is why the Vietnam draft, despite the many people who evaded service, garnered enough men to fight this war.

Their misuse, wasting their honorable commitment, played a big role in how these values themselves would soon be destroyed in the larger cultural war. Our best fighters were away for much of that one, and I frequently wonder how differently it might have gone were they here at home when needed.

Chapter 12: Love Everything, Care for Nothing

It doesn't take much for freedom to begin to sound like anarchy. After all, the ultimate freedom would be to remove oneself from consequence, to hold no responsibility except to one's conscience, and to be beholden to no idea or duty beyond the momentary pleasure. Such feelings could be genuinely liberating for people, especially young people to seek out, in response to a society built upon order, obligation, and long-standing connections.

The 1960's questioned everything and kept nothing. Bolstered by the greatest material success up to that point in world history, the Baby Boomer generation which grew up in relative tranquility in the 1950's came into their own and rebelled against all their parents had fought to preserve. No stone was left unturned in a battle against inequity, which in many ways was a struggle against nature itself.

Life is not fair. People have unequal talents. Groups have imbalanced merit. Anyone using reason can see these things as clear as day. But the children of the flower generation followed the guidance of Marxists who glorified the exceptions, while debasing the traditional to find a greater equality. What they ended up seeking was peace through serenity – purchased by the decision to absolve themselves of all moral decision making other than to say all things must be equal and all groups must be considered.

There were benefits to this approach in terms of how it brought disparate groups of people in contact with one another. A highly segregated society was forcibly enmeshed both by government and civic demand, seeking to find a new resolution where every person could fit. The optimists claimed the culture of this new America would reflect a new prosperity for all people, but as would become even more evident in the passage of time, what could unite people proved decidedly more concrete and less ideal.

The potent combination of drugs and sexuality were at the vanguard of this revolution. If it felt good, then we could all enjoy the good life, and there was experimentation in many new ways. Trying new substances to gain insight into experience became a lifestyle and a rite of passage. People indulged deeply, some too much so, and lost themselves in the psychedelic haze. Fortunately, the government stepped right in with a level of public financial support ensuring anyone could live at a survivable minimum, which facilitated indulgence in fantasies as they turned to vices.

Virtue became obsolete as women moved toward a liberation that entailed their self-willing debasement where sex could be traded as any other commodity – an experience to be shared with as many people as possible. More on the women's revolution will follow, but it was during this time that flesh replaced commitment, and the culture of hook-ups first began its assault in earnest upon marriage and the traditional male/female partnership which is the bedrock of our civilization.

Woodstock was the exemplary demonstration of the age, where music lubricated these trends and millions of young men and women came out to realize themselves, a mass rebellion against all that had come before. Where their ancestors had fought, they would instead submit. Where their parents had ideas, they had feelings. Where past generations had duty, they would find their freedom. And they would not merely seek these things for themselves but would demand them from all future generations as well. Any attempt to exercise any harsh judgment would thenceforth be labeled as heresy and duly punished.

In the forest of feelings, the crime was to kill the buzz. It was impolitic to question the new people being brought in from the Third World because they were people too. It was rude to defend marriage as being so binary, because love was all that mattered. To want to keep what one earned was selfishness, and just like a hookah in the tent, money was to be shared.

The government was thrilled to embrace this wave of good feelings, as were all the power centers of society from banking, to corporations, and academia. They nobly offered to help, taking responsibility away from the individual, promising to meet each need of every group but the oppressive majority. Having surrendered such responsibilities, the Boomers liberated themselves to search for meaning through experience, a sensual form of decadence that spawned a novel dominant cultural pattern to serve for more than just their own generation.

Art tore at the traditional balance between nature and harmony, emphasizing the abstract and the obscure. Music ceased to celebrate culture, but instead became a force of destruction leading people toward more primal beats. Literature emphasized the individualized experience, celebrating the commonplace instead of an aspirational culture. Taken in unison, the art of the era encouraged the mundane and the admission of all to the carnival of delights, while discarding all that had preceded them.

Even a reactionary like myself will concede there was a degree of corruption and issues with traditional structures of authority such that this approach could have appeal. Yet, the duties and mores of a society are what maintain a civilization and a nation across generations. It had never been tried so clearly to embrace freedom from account as the social governance structure, but the closest historical examples are the late stages of empire where decadence reigned.

When people only care for themselves, as much as they superficially can relate to one another, a strange inversion happens where people begin to lose regard for one another. Like ships passing in the night, they can see one another, but have no meaningful interaction as they go their separate ways. Absent some shared purpose, often driven by a real and pressing concern, civil society breaks down and neighbors stop trusting one another. Taken to the most extreme, even the family breaks down where the parent(s) put themselves first and the children only seek escape. We became so free, so individualistic, that we had nothing to share but the space we occupied.

And when that happened, crime rose, and the state could now justify further growth for two reasons. Firstly, as the common culture built on common concern decays, people will seek out their own truths. The one America of 1950 gave way to an America of many colors first, and then genders, and other newly imagined categories. The many race riots of 1968 were a prolific and violent example, but they were not alone as the new overtook the old. Secondly, the majority then had to live in fear and suspicion, finding themselves relying more on the state as well, even as it worked against them, to protect them. The devil's bargain was struck: silence in exchange for protection.

It bears repeating that in a society with Freedom of Speech, that right was reserved so that we might intelligently question our government to maximize our liberty. But in current practice, exercising that freedom and the affiliated right to free association is constrained by the expectation we will not question those ideas which are required to keep the peace in a culture lacking unified traditions. This partially explains our obsession with metrics today, trying to put numbers to all things, because we're conditioned not to make qualitative judgments. The ultimate sin in America is to say my idea is better than yours, fashioned out of the Baby Boomer moment where they decided no one can ever know, and therefore nobody can judge anyone else.

Relativism is the death of reason. That is the heritage of the cultural revolution, and those who rebelled were so numerous and thorough they successfully isolated, incorporated, or eliminated the other currents of thought in society which could resist.

Churches back then went different directions, but America has moved in a steadily secular direction since the 1960's. Spirituality replaced religiosity, with ideas and experiences from a dozen different places replacing the admonitions and instructions about character which came from the Christian doctrine. Constrained now with the threat of losing their tax money for giving political voice to anything but the approved agenda, there were many congregations all too happy to settle for the thirty pieces of silver to ensure their survival, with other voices now exiled to the periphery.

The charitable orders which existed both with faith communities and on a more generalized civil basis now had competitors. Who would need a convent to care for the sick or a parochial school with the government guaranteeing to provide Medicaid and access to quality public education? Liberals embraced the progressive era and conservatives stopped giving to these organizations as their tax money was already predetermined to go toward giving government these duties.

Where we once had options and choices in our society, these were given over to the state so that we could search within ourselves for some deeper meaning. Encouraged by every vector of culture to indulge in every substance, vice, and means of self-destruction, the generation which rose up to destroy what had existed before them, retreated into contemplation and comfort. They would intervene only to protect their retreat, leaving behind watchdogs.

Universities launched this revolution under the auspices of free speech, speaking out against the injustice of the majority, and empowering students to uprise. But having taken down the old ways, they quickly transformed into defending their own new orthodoxy, a long and gradual road culminating in today's censorship and safe spaces, where reason itself is discarded in favor of settled solutions, the dogma of the ideal of equality, tranquility, and unanimity.

As metaphor, I can best describe their actions as a bit like when one has drunk too much and enjoys the perfect buzz. To stop drinking would end the feeling, and to drink too quickly would lead to instant sickness, but to drink just the right amount might buy a few more moment's bliss at the expense of a greater reckoning tomorrow. For a very long time, I believe we have been trying to take those extra drinks slowly, putting off responsibilities to tomorrow, and leaving ourselves with a dreadful accounting not far distant.

Because, as it turns out, not everyone who comes here believes in peace and tranquility. It turns out justice and equality were just the pretense for the Marxists and their allies whose radicalism has gone unquestioned for over fifty years. Now, we find new groups vying for dominance, all waiting just beneath the surface to finish what the Boomers started: The nihilistic drive to fundamentally transform society. Those whom they empowered and those whom they often chose above their own children, we must now reckon with as we see that having different cultures in one place is only an invitation to conflict, because not all truths are reconcilable.

Such struggle is inevitable, as it is not of the choosing of the majority who made the bargain to just keep working hard in exchange for protection. It was a foolish choice, as those to whom we gave such power used it to take away our strongest bonds to come together to organize.

The war against the natural did not end in the 1960's, but rather took on a new and even more virulent phase: The incitement of women against men, dividing not just families, but destroying the last and strongest bulwark by which we could care for ourselves. Using the language of freedom, the Women's Revolution began during the 60's but came to dominate the 1970's.

Chapter 13: The War of the Sexes – Both Sides Can Only Lose

Let us start this chapter by asserting a self-evident truth: Men and women are different. Neither is better than the other, and both are complementary to one another. Both research and practice have made it abundantly clear that men and women see the world in very different ways, and as politically incorrect as it is to observe this, these functions largely fit a more traditional role of the division of labor between men and women in reproduction and child rearing.

While allowing for differentiation for individuals, men tend to think more abstractly, more long-term, be less emotive, physically more powerful, and able to shift focus. Women tend to think more concretely, address immediate concerns, be aware of their feelings, be more comforting, and tend to be alert to recurring issues. In other words, men are built to protect and defend, and women are built to preserve and support.

For thousands of years, this basic understanding of men and women went unchallenged as this partnership formed the foundation of the family, enshrined in marriage, and recognized that a two-parent family offered the optimal support, usually within a larger generational context, to provide support to the entire clan and to the offspring specifically. The enduring strength of this model across cultures speaks testimony to its success, and even today statistics strongly suggest two parent families provide greater opportunities for children than single parent alternatives.

All this is relevant to speaking about women's liberation because while the story told in the public eye is about the emancipation of women from their world of drudgery and housework, a very different narrative is equally valid. What if the purpose of women's liberation was not to enhance freedom or equality, but rather represented a flanking attack on the single most important institution which offered counterbalance to the growing moral and legal authority of the state: To attack the family?

What did the women's revolution accomplish? Instead of having a society where our expectation was that women would raise children and care for their young, a natural impulse to which many women aspire, women are instead taught that to only be a mother is insufficient. They are taught they can compete with men, but this goes even a step further to argue they should go out into that world, working solely for their own desires instead of investing energy into the home.

The movement started in the 1960's with sexual liberation. Where women were once encouraged to handle themselves modestly, the liberation upon them denuded them of their dignity and instead encouraged them to indulge in pleasures of the flesh. With birth control readily available and abortion legalized as an option against any unwanted mistakes, sex was increasingly separated from the very idea of procreation. A sacred act became profane entertainment, and as sex became commonplace, its import diminished.

Free love quickly devolved into cheap sex. Whereas women were once able to use their sexuality as a natural connection to men, their desire for approval and affection would lead down a path where instead of this liberated sexuality being empowering, it left many women only searching and wanting more. Men and women became more distant from one another, meeting to satisfy their instinctive physical needs, but seeing each other more warily as their worlds diverged.

Work became an arena for competition. Encouraged to go to work, women left their homes in numbers unseen before historically to meet the social challenge of liberation, to prove they were equal to men. In many ways, they met that challenge, because plenty of women succeeded remarkably in the incipient post-industrial economy where their administrative skills were effective. But, whereas the old system had one person, almost always the man, working to make enough money to sustain his wife and family, the new system required both parents to work, each making less as the labor supply swelled with wages dropping accordingly.

More importantly, with both parents now at work, who would be raising the children? Absent a mother at home to show love and concern for her children, those with kids saw the first generations raised by radio, television, and later the Internet. Government-approved institutions would be paid to care for children who were not their own, and the state reached into our lives ever earlier with preschool programs. In the search for our own fulfillment, yet again, the state would reach into our families even earlier.

Men and women started out as collaborators, distinct and indispensable to one another to realize our shared futures. Now, we would be turned into competitors, part of yet another struggle to reshape society away from what it had been and into something new. Such confusion about outcomes further weakened our shared culture and created a wedge between men and women that has festered to this day.

With women acting stronger and independent, men lost their sense of identity also. No longer permitted acts of chivalry and gallantry, men stopped showing the same regard and courtesy toward women. Instead of symbols for inspiration, women were transformed into objects of desire, with considerable help from a now nascent pornography industry that wrapped itself in the same language of liberation to peddle flesh in place of spirit. With sex trivialized, children subsidized, and the workplace becoming the battle of the sexes, the real loser was neither men nor women: It was the family.

The question we all should ask is: Was it worth the sacrifice? Were money, material assets, and these good times worth having children who grew up learning that material goods were more important than time and affection? Some parents worked hard and long hours to provide the toys pushed so frequently on television, while others basically neglected their children willfully, yet the damage done is strangely similar. In a sad irony, we learned this lesson: Stuff matters more than people and time, and that is how we must live if we wish to be successful.

Feminists might balk at how these arguments are being presented because of the assumption being made the primary purpose of women is to bear young. But this is the nature of the species, with our highest obligation and sacred duty being to prepare those who follow us to have a better future, investing our time and energy into our children and their welfare, knowing that without them all our accomplishments only fade to dust. They lose sight of that inescapable reality in their short-sighted search for fulfillment and in chasing these illusory promises of contentment.

This general criticism is as applicable to men as it is to women, because in our embrace of an unremitting freedom, we have all neglected our responsibilities to the future and to ourselves. Men need to be better partners, rediscover their strength, and reach out to women to rekindle what still waits to be rediscovered. Women need to remember the miracle that they possess to give life and encourage it into a new universe of being. We once had this, in love and support, and in the last few generations it has been given away. All for stuff and vanity.

People deserve equal rights, but men and women are not equal. Men and women can never be equal, and why would any sane person try to make a man into a woman or vice-versa? The only reason imaginable to my mind is to try to separate them, to put them forever at war with one another, and only those who sought to destroy a society and a culture would want that.

If this sounds crazy, consider how far we have come in the current day where now men identify as women and the opposite and any of numerous different artificial and frankly insane genders? We break what is natural, time and again, and impose what is fake. As we do so, and we disconnect ourselves from reality, we lose agency over our own lives and the ability to select our own futures.

Such freedom as we are offered is just a dream, a momentary respite from reality spawned from the 1960's where we were told we could be whatever we wanted. Perhaps it is even true in some subjective sense, but the cost of such indulgence is not only the loss of all we ever had, but the ability to shape our future and aspire to anything better for ourselves. Because if we are all so unique, we must forever be alone, and it is into this deep dislocation we have slowly and self-righteously drifted.

We consider ourselves tolerant, but that word denotes a lack of concern and passive indifference. We co-exist without cooperation, because we have no common truth. We are free, but we are lost. Because the price of giving up all we were is that we also surrendered all those beliefs we once held dear. And to this day, we still struggle to fill that hole with temporary bursts of feeling or crass material comforts.

We call that success, but ironically, isn't that the triumph of the Marxists? They always said happiness would come with material wealth and when man was liberated from his old beliefs. It's funny how with so many choices, we have truly never been so isolated and separated. This has hurt all people, but for women more than most as they have been forced to become something they never were in the name of progress and their so-called liberation.

Chapter 14: How the Heartland Became the Rust Belt

Whatever cultural upheaval was happening in the 1960's and into the 1970's, America was still the dominant industrial power on the planet. Having avoided the devastation that wracked much of the world during World War II, the positive side-effect of creating and maintaining the national security state was that the factories had been kept humming. Rebuilding through first the Marshall Plan and then many smaller efforts later ensured continual demand for American goods.

For a generation, those who fought in World War II earned peace for themselves in the proverbial suburbia with white picket fences. Jobs paid a decent income, enough for a man to feed his family and to save up a little for vacations and what not. Inflation was happening, but it hadn't accelerated yet like it would when Nixon dumped the gold standard. Life was relatively good from the financial perspective.

Such an economic foundation could have served as the basis around which organization against the cultural movements which so destabilized society coalesced, but these supports were also eroded. In an act of either generosity or folly, America basically surrendered our economic dominance by a series of decisions that weakened the middle class and pushed them toward government dependency.

A changing labor force was at the center of the issue. Women now flooded into the workplace. After the repeal of the 1965 immigration act, cheap labor came in from overseas. The civil rights movement brought minorities into new job sectors, and the combined weight of all these actors depressed wages but they also politicized economics in a way they had never been before.

The old American ethic had been about having the best man for the job, and the assurance there was a place for all who worked hard. Unions existed, but their purpose was rooted directly in the interests of their members to ensure pay, benefits, and reasonable work hours. Increasingly from the 1960's onward, unions would become political creatures in an even more explicit way.

As an aside, it's worth pointing out that while unions were allowed to take money from their members without consent or choice, and then use that money for political bargaining and promotion of candidates and parties, churches were denied that same right by the government with voluntarily given contributions. It's an early example of how the government continually worked to ensure only those entities which wanted expanded government control would be permitted the functional ability to use their free speech.

In exchange for generous benefits, the unions were glad to sign up with the progressive agenda, and work suffered as a result. Productivity lapsed throughout the industrial heartland as hiring practices shifted from bringing in the best person for the job to this new idea that diversity best reflected our strengths. Not only was it encouraged, but it was essentially enforced because once someone was brought into a firm from any of the rapidly widening protected classes, firing them for cause was an invitation to fight a discrimination law suit in a judiciary which had been stacked with liberal justices.

Businesses tried to adapt, but as they failed because of bureaucratic strictures, they left. The first great post-war migration of capital was from the North and industrial Midwest where mills closed shop in Union states and went down south. Parts of the old Confederacy which had languished in comparative poverty since Reconstruction one hundred years earlier were now getting mills in places like Alabama and Tennessee where lawmakers offered right to work states.

I lived in Pittsburgh for nearly 10 years. You can still drive down certain boulevards today where you see these huge mills which once existed, and which now are abandoned heaps of rust and scrap. People talk of how they made better money forty years ago, and the life that was lost. A big part of it was social programming forcing industry to become less productive, to the benefit of neither the worker nor the owner, but to realize some goal of an imagined great society. Equality always leads to poverty. Where unequal people had independence thanks to honest work, the welfare rolls predictably swelled as equalized people had no other recourse besides stagnation or migration.

Once businesses became detached from their traditional communities, it wasn't long before business leadership no longer balanced the imperative to turn a profit with a sense of social commitment. We will cover this much more in depth in the booming 1980's, but this is the time when the community/business bond shattered and capital flight happened. Foolish laws catalyzed the action, but individual and corporate greed sent so much of our wealth overseas, never to return.

We see this even more clearly today where we measure the value of a business solely through corporate earnings, instead of realizing business was always the center of the Main Street community and the way each generation assured their towns and cities survived. Towns ended up hollowed out because the money had left, and while the numbers might add up better on an overall balance sheet, what damage did the departing businesses leave in their wake?

Chapter 15: Trading Gold for Oil Just to Watch It Burn

At the same time this was happening, President Nixon was able to draw the United States out of Vietnam, but he made the fateful decision to remove America from the gold standard. Describing currency and monetary policy is often not the most interesting topic for people to understand, but it is vitally important because it plays a central role in what each of us earns and what our money can and cannot do.

Money had traditionally been a form of collateral – a promissory note. One dollar in paper was equal to a certain amount of silver, gold, or some other tangible asset of value. The quantities floated in accordance with the shifting value of goods, but at least, there was the confidence the dollar had some value, and could be redeemed for such specie if required.

Having money tethered to a certain quantity of assets, which was gold in this instance, served as a check in many ways against government spending. Funds needing to be raised had to be gathered through tax dollars inviting public scrutiny and skepticism. Both accountability and prudence were more likely to be exercised, but the downside was the dollar was very attractive to foreign investors. They'd buy the dollars up, and they would then seek to trade them in for gold. This is precisely what happened when the American gold supply shifted from control of the Treasury to the Federal Reserve Bank and to other institutional actors.

It's easy to miss a heist masquerading as a transaction, but what essentially happened is certificates worth gold and silver were redeemed leaving us with money that would thenceforth have nothing but paper value, called fiat currency. Having zero intrinsic worth, the dollar of today is only assured by the faith people place in the ever-expanding American government. Investors found such a concept less thrilling, and from the early 70's onward, inflation has roared forward.

When you see how much more things cost today even though we hear all the time how technology and logistics improvements make products cheaper and processes more efficient, do we ever stop to think why everything costs more? The simplest rationalization people seem to embrace is that novelty adds cost which can be true, but even more fundamental is that our money has become worthless. A penny in 1910 could purchase the same quantity of goods a dollar could in 2010. The value of that other $.99 was shuffled away, partially to inflation, but also to other stakeholders.

Oddly enough, for as much pain as this would cause throughout the entire decade of the 1970's where interest rates jumped into the double digits making loans insanely unaffordable, neither the government nor the banks were unhappy about the development. Now that the only value of money was how much could be printed, the capital restrictions upon how much money could be either spent by the government or printed by the banks disappeared. The only actual restriction was they needed consent by the public to keep the paper rolling, and due to a combination of ignorance about how money worked and a desire to avoid the reckoning such a bubble inevitably must create, everyone went along with the scam. They still do today – it's called quantitative easing and the national debt. These are numbers so huge people can only mentally shrug them off.

But the American government did not just accept that paper money would be worthless because of the facts of the situation. Instead, the government went ahead and made sure that where laws once worked, muscle would be used instead to ensure the dollar retained some value. Thus, began in earnest our adventuring in the Middle East. OPEC (Oil Producing Exporting Countries) is a cartel with which people might be familiar as they control oil production to ensure the price remains at a certain mutually agreed upon level. They are often presented as foes, especially when they have limited production to influence policy, but what people miss is they're also in many ways a function of American policy.

OPEC made a devil's bargain with the United States wherein they would control the oil supply but would agree to only accept American dollars for purchasing. So, if Japan wanted to buy oil from Saudi Arabia, they could not make their purchase in Yen directly, but instead had to purchase, hold, and spend American dollars to import the oil needed for their economy to run. As oil made the world turn, countries had no choice but to purchase American paper money for liquid transactions and American treasuries to fund our ever-growing debt and expanding budget.

To ensure no one got other ideas, American military power served as the guarantor to enforce these contracts, explaining why we would start our perpetual drama of getting involved in military issues in countries like Iran, Iraq, Kuwait, and Saudi Arabia. We propped up dictators wherever we could because if we didn't, our dollar would crash. Although expensive oil could hurt our businesses, oil being too cheap would destroy our government as our dollar would run away with hyperinflation.

We went from a country that produced goods to one which basically served as mob enforcer for a pyramid scheme. Where we used to make products, we now shifted toward financial instruments and interventions. Where productive industry was once the hallmark of America, we began the process of surrendering the ability to make what was real for command of what was imaginary. Culture, finance, entertainment, and ideas would be our exports. And if people didn't like them, there was always the stick of Americans willing to rally patriotically once more around the flag.

Power became even more centralized, and as the elites in government circles corresponded more with foreign powers for their success and survival, we see how globalism took another jump forward. Institutions and relationships would determine the future, now having decoupled the financial destiny of a nation from both the tax base and therefore the political consent of the people. Such freedom is always somewhat illusory, but no one dared pierce the veil.

But for the people working in the 1970's, it was a hard time. Our work ethic was lost, our ability to produce for ourselves was severely diminished, and families had to cope with the idea of working more to earn less. That was never the American way, but culture began scoping that into some sort of perverse challenge, forever asking us to do more with less instead of realizing the ability to do more because we earned it.

Chapter 16: How I Learned to Be Rich and Love the New Culture

If the decade preceding was full of pessimism and realism, the 1980's represented a boom time for America. President Reagan brought the sunny disposition of an actor to Washington for the first time and expressed life with the same clarity we would expect from the silver screen. Making money was good, America would become wealthy, and we labeled our enemies as such in crisp dialectical language of good and evil, a traditional favorite.

In many ways, the new wave was a respite from the struggles and cultural upheaval that had dominated America since Kennedy's murder. Unity was emphasized in place of disunity, a consolidation of the gains the cultural revolution had wrought. Equality and opportunity were presented as values working in cooperation, all in the shared promise that Americans could now all be rich.

Scarcity has always been the primary constraint against economic growth and the source of value for any given item or service. The idea of perpetual growth was not novel, but it had never been considered as a serious possibility before the boom decade. Now that government could essentially spend as much as it wanted with the remainder being national debt to be put off for some later date well into the future, and with money having no constraints other than how much force the state was willing to apply, the American hyperpower went into overdrive in indulging our imaginations to create new wealth.

Stocks boomed, and regulations were pushed aside. Banks which had once been constrained to only invest in one field or set of instruments were encouraged to explore possibilities. Products like the derivatives that would become so infamous in the 2007 bailout debacle were innovated in the 1980's. Those who ran the stock market realized people just wanted new ways to make money, and though they found suitable language to conceal the deeper truth, they basically served as bookies for a nation ready to gamble.

Some organizations would want safer bets, like the pension funds that were transferred from the public sector of bonds and treasuries and put into the blue chips and AAA rated funds to realize a better rate of return. America truly became a business where the lines between private and public, not just in terms of personnel, but also financially, became ever blurrier and more fluid. The government had to protect the market because the market could collapse the government. The Fed and the State had long developed this arrangement, but when it worked, everyone was excited to see their investments keep multiplying and good days finally come into being.

We found plenty of places to spend. The old standby of defense contracting was lined up at the ready to provide jobs and dividends as we pushed our old Communist adversary into a spending battle to see who could buy better toys to destroy the other. With the propaganda machine at full bore for basically the entire decade raising a whole generation to fear Russians, Americans were glad to invest in their forces and wherever the state required. We supported Iraq against Iran, before we would support Kuwait against Iraq. But we always supported whomever took dollars for oil.

Industry stopped being about production – a dirty business better left to foreigners – and instead became about wealth. We brought people into this country in huge numbers, some legally but many who came of their own volition through the southern border entering agriculture and other service sector fields. The rationale promoted was these were jobs beneath American hands, and so we would need new Americans to undertake the dirty work. Opportunity was said to be more important than culture, and perhaps due to fatigue from the many cultural battles, too many were happy to acquiesce.

Reagan passed the first great amnesty bill, legalizing millions of workers in what was promised to be the one and only time this would happen. You might have noticed a pattern where politicians love to make and break their promises regarding wars, taxes, and anything else, but the precedent was now set. If one wanted to work, coming to America was warranted, and the laws would catch up to the reality on the ground. Where immigration policy once was rooted in culture and identity, it was now becoming a function of labor demands for a society which was decoupling wealth from work.

People can only fight so long before they submit. Although a person does not always know their breaking point, the modern society by this point had become overwhelming in its ability to put pressure on people and then offer release. Television was in its most dominant age before the onset of the Internet, where message control was still held through just a few networks. The news made people feel worried and then comedy provided relief. We were told all people should be judged just on how good they were and made to laugh at our differences to bring us together.

They could have just as easily shown the numerous examples of how diversity led to many unhappy outcomes. The epidemic with cocaine usage, felt most heavily but not exclusively in the black community, was just one example. Crime skyrocketed as people wanted to embrace the good feeling of the time, and drug culture which had simmered since the 1960's in the relatively benign form of marijuana and the strange experiences of psychedelics morphed into something much more harmful and dangerous: Crack.

A strange irony is the same process used to undo white families a generation earlier, where drugs would be used against a social order now happened in the black communities. The black family was decimated by drug usage, and for those who bothered to pay attention to scandals like Iran-Contra, it became increasingly evident that our own Deep State was heavily involved in the drug trade. It was a way for them to launder money worldwide and fund their own black budget in violent places like Nicaragua and Columbia which were just dots on the map to most Americans.

But these real issues were swept under the rug in many ways and used as further means to accelerate the cultural divide between races. While the surface current was toward unity, pushed by television and designed to keep Americans from becoming too restive as our eyes were focused on the red threat abroad, the divergence in culture became clear in the 1980's. Mass music is one example, as different groups began speaking of their different truths of life and their aspirations.

Rap emerged before it evolved into hip hop. Various Latin sounds started entering our radios. Country, as a white counterculture, started to break into the mainstream. And rock, which had been the music of the land since the 1960's, enjoyed its last hurrah as it became incorporated into the mainstream as an enshrined statement of the cultural revolution. Music can be enjoyed by anyone, naturally, but the point is the separation by group was accelerating. The language of unity gave cover to the next evolution of warfare which we now face today: The resumption of racial interests.

In good times, however, it was easy to hide these problems. What we didn't want to deal with, we left to others, and for the first time you saw foreign competitors offering better and cheaper products than America. Japan was the threat in this period, with people thinking they would be building the entire future. Of course, time would show how their inflationary bubble basically tanked their economy and has made it so bad that people must be paid to procreate, a problem the Europeans would later come to share.

But that didn't matter. The future only mattered in as much as we were optimistic and could enjoy it. Savings and loan crises were examples of people who made bad decisions, not a warning the whole system was unsustainable. Credit cards lined the pockets of the working man and now woman, and if money hadn't been saved to pay for something, it didn't matter because everyone could share a piece of the prosperity. A little interest paid into the system didn't seem so bad when growth was outpacing the bills due.

Writing in these more cynical days, it's easy to make that period seem ridiculous, but I remember growing up during the time thinking this was a period of hope. My parents seemed to feel the same. After years of anguishing through poverty, stagflation, huge interest rates, and the like, the 80's emulated the 50's as another moment of calm before the storm. But oddly enough, even the storm which would emerge would be a moment of triumph.

The fiction upon which we based our spending created a momentous real-world result. Thanks to a combination of economic wrangling, their own folly in getting bogged down in Afghanistan, and a growing desire for freedom expressed by many people, the Evil Empire came crashing down. America had won the great battle of our time by 1991, prompting heady scholars to claim the end of history had finally been reached. For those who grew up subjected to years of programming where victory over Eurasia would be the great goal, imagine how rewarding that must have felt.

Chapter 17: Defeat Through Victory – A State Seeking Purpose

From 1945 until 1991, the world was defined by its bipolarity. When America formed NATO, the Soviet Union formed the Warsaw Pact. When the Soviet Union went into space, America went to the Moon. Each side used the other as a measuring stick, going tit for tat in different fields of achievement and spending, each amassing an empire which sustained and built up its elites.

For all the ideological differences between the two factions, the communists and capitalists followed the same pattern that repeats with disturbing frequency throughout European and American history where we fight those closest to us. Fighting with the same fervor as Protestants once opposed Catholics, and for much the same reason – for the health of the state – the leadership of the two groups was less different than the people who supported them.

Both countries had built huge bureaucratic apparatuses which were heavily invested in both the military and various secret service and intelligence agencies. Both countries were obsessed with material status and accepted tacitly that their elites would make those determinations even as they paid lip service to democratic ideals of serving the people directly. The leadership was well-educated, secular, calculating, and believed the whole world could be fit into one system.

The American system offered more individual freedom in how labor was expended. The Soviet system promised greater equality at the floor. America transitioned toward offering freedom of cultural expression in exchange for political indifference, and in that action, they were able to outlast the Communists. It turned out that so long as the rituals were followed, people cared far less about politics than having economic status and cultural liberty. Provided these two were maintained at a respectable level, the bureaucrats could operate with minimal oversight and hindrance.

As the Soviets repressed these impulses, they saw Germany fall away first with the Berlin Wall coming down in 1989. Unwilling and unable to repress as brutally as they had done in Czechoslovakia in 1968, the other occupied countries of Eastern Europe quickly folded away from the Soviet Union. By 1991, the military organized unsuccessfully to stop the bleeding, but upon their failure the old Russian Empire collapsed into different components, and far more suddenly than anyone could have imagined, the unipolar world was upon us and the West was triumphant.

Of course, it wasn't quite that simple. China had shown one clear example, in their ruthless suppression at Tiananmen Square, that force could still hold power. An authoritarian bureaucracy which could deliver economic progress and an improving quality of life, often presented in nationalist garb to provide some flavor, survived fine in many places. In the Russian scenario, the inability to sustain the ruble after their failed incursion into Afghanistan and the resultant financial hardship proved too much to bear. But China avoided these errors and remains strong today.

What we discovered in considering three different scenarios: The American, the Russian, and the incipient Chinese, would become the basis of Globalism 1.0. Moving toward the proverbial New World Order quoted by U.S. President George Bush, the idea was to place institutions above countries so a permanent over-class could form between the elites of the various countries. The democracy of nations model from the United Nations worked perfectly here as double think, where you had the formalism of democracy with the least democratic representatives imaginable.

The bankers would run the economies going forward, with the World Bank and International Monetary Fund rushing throughout the world to provide guidance and insight. The same people who controlled the Federal Reserve and similar other banks outside the United States promoted their neoliberal ideas of free markets and unlimited growth. Considering how well it had worked for the United States, it was easy to sell this to not just the Second World, but the developing world where assets were brought under control of finance, guaranteed by the force of America.

Previous wars had required the justification of opposing the interests of a national power, but humanitarian intervention made a massive comeback in the 1990's as the idea of universal human rights was proffered to extend the cultural liberties which lent themselves so nicely to economic domination and political submission. Always available as a threat, the idea of intervening to save people was selectively applied to benefit both American and globalist influences.

Kuwait was liberated in 1992 because Saudi Arabia required that to protect the petrodollar. Serbia was bombed and fractured shortly thereafter not because of the carnage which post Yugoslavia left in the Balkans, but because it was the odd man out for future NATO expansion to recognize the dream of a single Europe. Each was sold to the public as a genocide in the making, and so America went into these places to enforce the new order by the bureaucrats, of the bureaucrats, and for the bureaucrats.

An alternative model which could have been tried based on earlier examples would have been the demobilization of the security state. There were indeed impulses in this direction as military bases were closing and the question of ending NATO was discussed. A great number of Americans were ready to disengage from the arms race, especially as the humanitarian interventions left sour tastes in the mouths of many. Somalia is a perfect example where a mission to feed people only empowered warlords and radicalism.

The formative years of the global consensus were disruptive precisely because they lacked the clear divisiveness that had defined not only the Cold War, but much of human history. While that would change after 9/11 where Islam became the perfect justification for any future intervention and the clash of civilizations began, it was the networking that happened in this era that laid out the basic structure for the years to follow.

Elites shifted away from nationalism and the interests of their respective countries, and instead aligned with their class standing across borders. They encouraged open immigration everywhere as means to not just create economic growth, but also to increasingly homogenize culture to reduce conflict. Their belief is that having a single people with a single culture and single economic system could realize Fukuyama's much mocked "End of History".

In fairness, there are some very well-educated people who believe that is the purpose of the entire globalist project. Ranging from neoliberals to neoconservatives, and from institutionalists to transhumanists, their basic theory is that war has become so destructive that humanity must be modified from its basic natural impulses of tribal identity and individual expression to something less potent.

The open border program is supposed to make people's jobs dependent upon one another. That was the rationale behind NAFTA which both parties in America ended up endorsing, despite the opposition of most Americans, and which has inexorably linked the American, Canadian, and Mexican economies. It destroyed the last of American manufacturing as well as Mexican agriculture, all in the name of efficiency and unity. People of very different cultures were forced together by policy, leading to interchange but also conflict.

This was no accident and done not just for economic reasons. Actions like this, which we see accelerating today in Europe and which were very much expedited prior to the Trump election in America, are designed to blend identity away into something meaningless. Positive social identity is now attached to blending identity, to tolerance and diversity, and toward conformity rather than uniqueness. We're being engineered to be indistinct from one another in what is probably the greatest social engineering project of all time.

But people deserve to know this is what is happening. They deserve to know their nations are being intentionally reduced away from their values, and individuals are slowly being stripped of the context not just to exercise, but even understand their essential liberties. We are being made to be individuals in a global network, a hive if you will, instead of free citizens of sovereign nations. As I think of it, it's the triumph of quantity over quality and the latest effort to fulfill Marx's predictions.

The end game of Marxism was always the belief that once the contradictions in society were worked out, an emergent synthesis of ideas would result whereby the communal nature of man as one unit would resume, and all would enjoy greater material status. That unspoken goal is the world we are now offered, beyond spirit and faith, detached from one another, but with optimal freedom at the cost of losing any connections based upon judgment. We can all be free, but only if we all are equal.

Given that such a program runs against both nature, a constant struggle of inequalities facing one another in contest, and our traditions, it is inevitable that dissidents would emerge. Underneath the surface of unity and ambivalence that represented the 1990's, there was also the beginning of a movement to oppose the global order underway.

Chapter 18: Discontents and the State Against Them

As the scale and scope of what was being put into place increased, so too did the opposition. Three major efforts come to mind, although there were also other smaller and regional efforts no less worthy of consideration. As people saw that the peace dividend at the end of the Cold War did not offer any hope of return to the smaller government promised for years and enshrined in the Constitution, they got organized and expressed their dissent.

Within the Republican Party, the efforts of Pat Buchanan and others who would come to be called paleoconservatives rose up to challenge the establishment orthodoxy represented by Bush 41, former CIA Director, and longtime hatchetman for the Deep State. He spoke about the importance of identity and morality, and intelligently projected where the trends of population replacement and displacement might lead. Long before the Tea Party was a thing, his candidacy pushed the same ideas which would rise again and again, stifled in an age where television remained ascendant and where activists hadn't yet figured out how to effectively work through the GOP primary process.

While TV viewers are told primaries exist to provide democratic governance for the citizenry, nothing could be further from the truth. They are how the parties control their candidates, marginalizing those whom they deem to be too far on the fringe, which in practical terms equates to those the donor class won't support. Although some people donate to campaigns for ideological reasons, most of the largest institutional donors take a far more transaction-based view of their dealings with the business world, and so they purchase both sides and explain the sell out as moderation and consensus.

Within the primaries, the rules are often structured in a way to preserve a certain limited range of outcomes. Whether through caucuses which require people to travel sometimes great distances to vote, or the even less helpful system of super-delegates in which party hacks are given equal weight to huge numbers of citizen voters, the goal of the process is to promote the party, make money for the political hangers on, and ensure the right candidate wins. In 2016, Hillary Clinton demonstrated how thoroughly the system gets played in how the entire Democratic National Committee worked to screw Bernie Sanders with dissenting voices like Seth Rich dying under mysterious circumstances.

But 1992 was a pivotal year for more than Republican resistance, as the first viable third-party candidate since the turn of the century arose in Ross Perot. His Reform Party and candidacy through Larry King offered a preview of what it might take to break through the media blockade: A direct message spoken simply, in this case opposition to the North American Free Trade Agreement (NAFTA) and repeated often appealed across party lines. Americans believe in sovereignty and in taking care of our own people, our nation first. The weight of votes on both sides has always been in that position, but for different reasons, the parties have always worked to undermine that weight.

For the right, the fascination with cheap labor has been used cynically by the Chamber of Commerce to turn a blind eye toward illegal immigration, support visas for anyone who wants to enter, and to deregulate in such a way that anything can be off-shored. Their greed – much more than the virtues publicly expressed – represented the GOP, whose defense of their beliefs could never be counted on so much as their avarice.

For the left, they saw in the emerging minority populations a voter population that fit perfectly into the long-term project to gain power by radicalizing those groups against the majority. Illegals began their transformation from a law enforcement issue threatening American workers, most commonly the low wage citizens who voted Democrat, to undocumented citizens whose diversity represented a positive counterbalance to our biased perspective. It's not surprising the Establishment worked against the interests of the people who supported them. They discarded the rural whites who gave them power in the 30's, the poor blacks who gave them power through the 60's, and should demographics change again, have no doubt they will change loyalties again.

Both parties are just a means to an end in enforcing their shared orthodoxy. Open borders, open immigration, open philosophy: War against value itself, lifted from the Marxist dreams of the 1960s, where tolerance for all things takes the place of actual reasoning and judgment.

Then, as now, an authentic message cuts right through the racket and Perot was making great progress. A toll-free number and volunteer army came into being just before the dawn of the Internet era, and he had every opportunity to win and preserve America. Then, for reasons which have never been fully explained, he chose to drop out. He re-entered the race later, but the moment was lost, and his late re-entry only served to grease the skids for the corrupt Clinton machine to first come to power.

People have often speculated about why Perot dropped out of the race despite the obvious success he was enjoying. No public reason was ever given, but there were rumors whispered for many years regarding threats made against his family if he were to continue. There is no way to verify any of these accusations absent Perot sharing them himself, but if protecting a trillion-dollar agenda requires derailing only one man, it seems obvious there would be many willing to serve in such capacity.

The rise in conspiracy thinking took off in earnest during the 90's as Americans struggled to reconcile a reality whose facts did not fit the provided narrative. When unions argue the influx cheap labor will create jobs, businessmen say they will create wealth by moving factories overseas, and politicians claim wars make peace, is it surprising such double-think would inspire massive disbelief?

Recognizing the cognitive dissonance, media in the pockets of the elite tried to marginalize those who asked critical questions by branding them as conspiracy theorists, a somewhat derogatory and dismissive term. In pop culture, they were portrayed such as they were on shows like X-Files, a radical fringe who held improbable assertions like aliens controlling humanity. Such ideas were pushed to muddy the waters, so that more genuine questions might be more easily ignored, like: who was controlling our government and what agenda did they have?

If you were to listen to AM radio late at night, and to a program like Art Bell, you might learn a great deal that didn't fit the narrative. Before InfoWars there was Coast 2 Coast, a show which covered some topics which were unlikely, but also which offered a gateway into a world where citizens still questioned the government. Videos were out there to be seen about ex-KGB agents speaking of how Marxists ran the West as much as they had the old USSR, and how they had infiltrated the universities to shape the minds of children. These were not the sexy videos, about money laundering, drug wars, and political infiltration. But time has shown these concerns were prescient.

The problem with conspiracy theories is that they are difficult to prove. For instance, the narrative which says Bill

Clinton came to power as a Rhodes scholar could sound something like this. Cecil Rhodes was responsible for plundering much of the wealth of Africa and for the predicament of South Africa, a country actively being erased of its white settlers, today. Clinton was selected because of his charisma and talents to run Arkansas, blessed by the support of a helpful and wealthy establishment. Despite many questionable scandals of both the personal variety, as well as financial actions like Whitewater, the press protected him as a made man, easier to control. The drug shipments flying in out of Mena for the Agency were just one example.

And both he and his wife have always managed to stay one step ahead of the law, perhaps because that is who protects them. When the documents for the case against them ended up in Oklahoma City, that building happened to be destroyed in one of the worst attacks on our soil up until 9/11. A potential disaster, just as in the case of LBJ, was turned into an opportunity by the crisis. Clinton served two terms, shielded by the media, and protected by his Deep State allies. That's a different way the Clinton years could be seen with ample evidence to support such assertions.

Of course, the trick of the question is being able to prove what you say and considering that the same people who bankroll our government also control media and academia, it doesn't pay to have these questions published or ideas explored. Instead, saying the wrong thing – then as now – turns your career into a black hole where legitimate inquiry is either derided as baseless superstition or worse, cast aside as prejudicial whenever possible. In short, those in control cannot be talked about, because those in a position to talk about them are already on board.

In the Internet age, this monopoly has broken somewhat with subsequent scandals, but it has always been a struggle to make people think contrarily to whatever the dominant narrative happens to be. Leaving aside the time commitment and intellectual labor it takes to ask these questions, let alone string them into a somewhat coherent narrative, there are real consequences to dissent. It's axiomatic that most people will not choose to pay those consequences provided they can enjoy an acceptable standard of living and freedom, and so we complain and wonder, but never really investigate.

The third and final way resistance took root in the 1990's was the idea that if we just left politics alone, politics would leave us alone. America has worked despite many contradictions because we started as an untamed frontier where people who did not like a way of living could usually find a different place to live and seek their own expression. As laws closed in to limit the freedoms people wanted to express, with Federal agencies granted and exercising new powers, the space for such departure steadily shrank.

The transition began with government ignoring the sovereign citizens who chose to defend their liberties like freedom of speech and the right to bear arms in seclusion, to targeting them as potential domestic terrorists. The sorry events of Waco and Ruby Ridge in which law enforcement descended upon people like an avenging army inflamed tensions throughout rural America, where Janet Reno, the FBI, and now other police agencies began their militarization in earnest. SWAT teams began to dot the land.

Social unrest like the LA Riots, citizen resistance, and then the Oklahoma City Bombing (which warrants much more critical analysis than it has been given), joined together to create the justification for turning police whose primary role had always been to serve as peace officers, into the masked forces we now see so commonly as law enforcement. These new masked forces act above and beyond the people who not only write their laws but pay their checks. Unsurprisingly, corruption ensued, and overreach and selective enforcement increased. The deplorable practice of civil asset forfeiture joined with a windfall of government money to fund such actions.

Thanks to the media, which ever took the side of authority, the Deep State was praised and supported, the establishment enacted their agenda, the borders were opened even wider, and now the patriots were called potential terrorists. Anyone who spoke too loudly about the Constitution was suspect, and right-thinking people learned not to ask questions lest they be deemed either a joke or a threat.

But that was the post Cold War period. Whereas during the Cold War everyone cared about what America meant, now you were not supposed to care too much about anything. To do so would be dangerous, and Americans could rest assure our government was in control. The victory of authority over liberty seemed to have reached a new pinnacle. And beyond the police state, biology itself would offer two new ways to enshrine the gains made: pharmacology and psychology.

Chapter 19: The Doctor is In and Sanity is Out

What is normal? It's a question with which our society seems obsessed, but which we never really solve. One definition could be the ability to fit into social norms without seeming to deviate from the range of acceptability. We emphasize the importance of this concept as part of fitting in and being able to co-exist but are sometimes blind to how we allow ourselves to be shaped to shifting definitions that change radically over time.

As late as the early 1990's, normal could have meant a two-parent family with children who were curious, creative, and comfortable in their identity as boys and girls on their way to becoming men and women. Jokes were still allowed about every group, laughing at the stupid things we all do, between ourselves and to one another, and we all understood this to be a means of reducing tensions. In many ways, it was healthier as there was both a sense of identity and means to reduce tension.

Although the process had begun much earlier, these natural inclinations started to be replaced by the professionalization of our psychological conditioning. Although this field of study had been around for many decades, never had social engineering penetrated so early and so deeply into our lives as it began to do in during this decade, and all in defense of a newly defined set of norms.

What was once called curiosity and hyperactivity, the seemingly natural desires of a child to explore the world and seek new stimuli as a means of learning, was re-branded as Attention Deficit Disorder (ADD). The few cases that perhaps merited some intervention to help children clinically unable to focus expanded quickly into a catch-all wherein the basic identity of what had been childhood for decades was turned into a diagnosed disorder. Drugs were dispensed with Ritalin flowing like water through the schools, and parents whose absence from their children made them overly eager were only too happy to consent.

I remember the paranoia inculcated into children like myself at an early age in so many ways. A seemingly noble program like DARE (Drug Abuse Resistance Education) taught stranger danger so many times that a whole generation grew up with anxiety about who to trust and to whom we could talk without risking our lives. It's impossible to know if that was the intent but building any sort of social institution which requires trust is difficult when you've been conditioned to respect authority, take your pills, and to be hesitant to even talk to anyone else.

Schools are but one example of the creeping reach of big pharma into our lives in ever-increasing ways. The promise of better living stopped being rooted in the satisfaction of work and the ability to effectuate social change beyond proscribed limits, and instead found realization in the great escape. Illegal drugs were profligate, but legal medication was no less available and served the same purpose for so many people.

Anti-depressants flooded the market, helping people to cope with lives that didn't make sense anymore. Presented as an act of kindness and a way to provide for better living in a rapidly changing world, is it not equally true they just served to dampen people's desire to change that which they did not want? It is far easier to just take a pill to wash away the worries of reality than to work to change what makes you unhappy.

Even more perversely, billions of dollars were made in putting out an unending succession of new drugs to amplify or mediate experiences, perfectly legal, but with little understanding of long term ramifications. SSRIs were dished out like candy, never considering the dependency they created and the psychoses that emerged should people try to liberate themselves from their use. Pain medication like opiates were the basis for the current heroin epidemic.

During this time frame, they sometimes called these people Prozac nation, but they were the people who checked out of the question of what the future should be. In finding a more satisfying present, they had doctors telling them this was the new definition of health as opposed to threatening the status quo with disruptive change. For the majority who had so often resisted changes to a society they did not understand and sometimes did not want, it was a gentle exit.

Many took it, and though the pharmacology continually evolves, many still take this path today.

It's a sign of a larger syndrome, where instead of curing the problems we face in our society or culture, we treat the symptoms. We either medicate away what we don't like or distract ourselves to oblivion, finding these easier than rooting out the sickness within. Things have never looked better on the surface, but how long can we live on illusion alone without seeking health at the core? No one wants to ask this question because it is upsetting and will lead to conflict, but we only delay the inevitable.

Chapter 20: Weapons of Mass Distraction

Addiction was reckoned a small price for the ongoing effort to offer new and novel escapes from reality. If drugs were one, then another was entertainment. Although there has always been a place for escaping the drudgery of life, never have there been so many options, tailored to the individual, but also satisfying the need for group identity.

Consider sports as one example. The camaraderie missing from social life, especially for men, found an ample surrogate in how we could cheer for our teams and follow our heroes who possessed the strength and achievement we were now denied. Where so many of us lived in a world now constrained by terms like efficiency and sustainability, they represented the primal urges toward exceeding boundaries which were both innovative but destructive to the emerging society. They were an outlet for aggression, and a massive distraction.

Where men once fought to preserve their values and their communities, they now dressed up in jerseys and cheered for a ball going down the field. The myth of the gladiator, conjured up from ancient Rome, remained as reliable as the circuses of yore in giving meaning to men who were being feminized in many ways. Taught to be tolerant, traditional masculinity was suppressed and metrosexuals were promoted as attractive.

Now, reality didn't conform to this new standard. Study after study across cultures show that women tend to prefer rugged men who express strength, and men prefer supple women who show their fertility. But changing the definitions of what represented attraction for men and women, bolstered by culture, set people binging off after even more drugs and diets to fit the style of the times, trying to realize the craziness mis-branded as progress that sought to compel men and women into being increasingly indistinct from one another. This trend would only accelerate until today's gender fluid perversion.

As all these new trends were explored, what became lost was what people were not doing. Increasingly, we defined ourselves even more radically than those who lived during the cultural tumult of the 1960's as personas apart from reality. We lost context of what it meant to control our society, foregoing not only the choice to shape our actual physical reality, but increasingly admitting that people possessed little interest, as we retreated into our subjective havens.

Much can be learned about a society by whom it deems as the most dangerous outcasts. We see here the hard push against violence as the greatest of disorders. From thenceforward, we would only be allowed to talk about our problems, and not do anything to change them. We would not have winners and losers, but instead we would have participants all worthy of awards. Distinction was too upsetting, so instead we would seek out unanimity.

If the goal of society is just to optimize harmony, which is what the Marxist vision sought as means to quell dissent, one could hardly imagine a better way of looking at the world. But if one wants to change the future, to assert their rights as an individual to stand against a world that doesn't make sense, these actions were design to render liberty into criminality.

Consider the unending war against guns as the perfect test case. Those who support gun rights do so because they believe the threat of mass violence is the last insurance against our government imposing laws against our will upon the people of this country without any restraint. As the saying goes, a government that fears its people will have liberty, but a people who fear their government will have tyranny. For a person who understands liberty, and that it exists in a perpetual tension which maintains equilibrium because people retain the power to defend themselves, retaining guns has always been the guarantee.

But for those who live in the world of harmony, where fantasy exists independent of any objective reality, weapons have always represented the harsh intrusion of nastiness into their fantasy. They shift their distaste onto guns like some wicked totem and those who possess arms as heretics. When the world doesn't conform to their vision, they seek to unmake reality and call it evil. A complicit government and culture, seeking always to fulfill the imperative to remove all restraints on its authority, is only too happy to agree.

Year by year, the Marxists are winning this fight. Not because they have taken the guns, but because through psychology and the control of language itself, they've changed what freedom means to people. Liberty seems abstract to people whose every basic need is covered by the state, whose creative and intellectual needs are entertained or medicated into submission, and who have been fully insulated through specialization from the consequences of reality. For those coasting along either willfully or helplessly, liberty would mean the death of their being, and so they oppose such violence as a tear against comfort – the peaceful rest of material progress.

The end game of equality – quantity over quality – always is nothingness. To care is to assert quality, to cause conflict, and to force struggle again and again. But if no one cares, everyone feels good, and all is taken care of, then the possibility arises for a victory over nature. In a morbid way, it's even a victory over nature itself, because we move beyond being creators of our own future and just gentle ourselves toward slow and peaceful destruction.

But we look for delays wherever we can find them and have become amazing at finding our escapes. Those who push for cultural and state transformation know this, and that's why they launched perhaps the most radical reformation project in the history of humanity: The Internet.

Chapter 21: You've Got Fail – The Dark Side of the World Network

It's hard to remember this now, but there was a world before the Internet and it was very different. Instead of mass communication where we knew instantly how people would respond to our every action, there was much more space to operate and uncertainty about what was acceptable. It's a funny thing in human psychology, but when we feel we are being watched, we start to behave differently to ensure we conform to social expectations.

This is important to remember when we consider the backbone for the Internet emerged not from some enlightened nonprofit, but instead in government funded research in Silicon Valley, and with direction and guidance from entities like DARPA (the Defense Advanced Research Projects Agency), which is basically a skunkworks for the military who seek out, test, and fund next generation research into all areas of warfare including most relevantly here, information warfare.

Think about when you go into a store and make a purchase as we all have, and you either see on the receipt or are told by some suggestive clerk there is a survey you are asked to complete to share information about your behavior. Often, some sort of inducement is offered for people to take the two minutes to answer a few quick questions, and very few people ever respond. Businesses would love to know what you want so they can encourage you to spend more on their products or services, but we historically were careful about protecting privacy about behaviors we didn't want to share.

With the advent of the search engine, the Internet has turned that world utterly upside down based upon a very neat trick. While it turns out we are very reticent to share our actual thoughts and desires with our fellow men, craving their approval more than knowledge or expression in most cases, if people are removed from this equation and replaced with an anodyne box, our every thought, dream, and hope are put forward earnestly seeking expression when we feel we are doing so privately and without consequence.

Think about what you've asked Google in your life. Am I correct in saying that there are many things you wouldn't want known publicly? Maybe it was something simple where you just had a basic question about knowledge you were never taught, and a quick answer helped. Perhaps you wanted to check in on what an old friend had been doing without having to seem creepy, which is why everyone both hates Facebook on some level and still has an account there. Or maybe social media is your vice, where information overload has created an addiction where information is needed sooner and more intimately. These are just a handful of the habits the Internet has created in how we behave, transforming who we are as people and removing the idea of privacy from our lives in so many radically different ways.

Those issues alone warrant an entire volume for consideration as we probably won't understand what this is doing to us until it is too late to revert to being individual sovereign citizens with the basic expectation of privacy, especially for young people who've never known a world where being offline just wasn't an option. But the Department of Defense was very aware of at least these potentials when they helped push these boxes into our homes where we could ask any question because they knew our words would echo into eternity.

Or at least, they would echo long enough along fiberoptic cables to be cataloged and recorded by a bureaucracy such as the NSA (National Security Agency) who knew how to listen. As information bounced freely around the world and into one jurisdiction and out of another, listening in became a technical problem where laws themselves could be arranged so interested parties could snoop into your desires. At one level, these could be used to anticipate your needs, just as the search engine bar does based on the input of millions of others to complete your thought before it is voiced. More darkly, such knowledge could also be used to implant false ideas and to shape minds, and in so doing shape the destiny of people themselves. We called it the Internet, but perhaps it should have been called Pandora instead of the radio network.

The National Security Agency (NSA) is the point agency for monitoring telecommunications in the US, although both the military and civilian agencies like the CIA must certainly have their own capacities out of fear for what having a singular actor having access to so much information about the people would allow. Social media could be used to instantly spread a narrative, where images would create a reality, and people would quickly build their perceptions around what was seen. The power to reshape reality now had the ultimate amplifier, a dangerous allure to those who could see its potential. It had never been easier to spread news and ideas, and that is the ultimate double-edged sword.

The Internet has opened worlds of new expression and has also broken a blockade against people being able to offer ideas blocked by existing institutions. While the establishment can and does use online actions to influence, suggest, and increasingly control how people think, resistance still happens at light speed, and we've seen firsthand how those who understand this technology have been able to offer a counter narrative. Absent the Internet, I wouldn't even try writing this book because there would be no hope that people might embrace the ideas which most publishers would be aghast to even consider.

We also have been able to find people who share our beliefs and create new networks based upon shared interest. This would seem to be a good thing, but the sword cuts both ways here. People are less engaged in real life than they have ever been as we can all now self-select our companions and live even more deeply within the fantasy which best suits our nature. There is real value in being forced to deal with people whose perspectives are different, but information technology increasingly allows us to settle into a safe comfort zone no less addicting than any other drug to our minds seeking relief from a society thrown into perpetual turmoil.

For someone like myself, a reformer, the digital world seemed to offer a retreat where ideas could be expressed, and people could be reached. Though that certainly happens, look also at how the Internet allowed the state a glimpse into a potential rebel, someone who rejected their culture, and how it facilitated their mass media to launch an attack against me, or any other dissident, where they can destroy a person's employment prospects forever with just a week of dedicated salvos. What we say lingers on, and in a world where so many are retreating into fantasy, what does that mean for a person's right to speak?

It's essential for the online world that we have these freedoms. But increasingly, whereas the early adopters of the Internet had the expectation that all but the most egregious offenses would be ignored, a slow but rapidly widening veil of censorship is being pushed. Terms like deplatforming, demonetizing, and now even criminalizing of thoughts themselves are segregating those who are welcome from those who are not welcome on those core sites where social ideas most quickly spread. #FakeNews is giving way to #FakeViews as the anonymity we rely upon hides the motives of all posting who are clever enough, meaning the person opposing you could just as easily be a bot putting out lines to shape a narrative for some paid actor or cause. We can trust nothing, and nothing and no one are real.

Relationships cheapen as both fear grows, and uncertainty rises. The Internet has become less a chance to network to shape reality, and instead a refuge for those in their discontent. Online activists listen to people like Snowden and Wikileaks, learning time and again through leaks how our platforms will be used against us. Yet, we cannot quit, because it is all we have, and we rationalize that the mere expression of an idea is equal to its realization, even if in our hearts we know that is not true. We do not fight because we have spoken. Our thoughts have been recorded, and having done at least something, our days continue.

Digital communications have made our world closer and made public what was once intimate. Open to such scrutiny, we have learned to conform and act as one. We make new friends in new places, but such superficial connections cannot replace the reality of working in actual reality. Some realize that, and to their credit, have learned to use these connections as a conduit to reach out into the larger world. Although harder, the Net allows that also, but the information war is a very real thing and it seeks to draw people away from the real into the trap of the virtual.

It is strange my own views should come off so pessimistically as I have learned so many things which otherwise would have been nearly inaccessible without the vast repository of information that sits at my fingertips, and which I've consulted frequently while drafting this exposition. Great information is out there to be had, but without context to find it, I fear it gets lost as a faint signal within a sea of noise. I worry, knowing how we think talking about a thing now is just the same as doing a thing. That's why our relationship with the Internet is love/hate.

The Internet gives us more, but everything becomes worth a little less. And if there is a fundamental duality between the forces at play, it is not just between those who seek to impose equality in a foolish or deceptive jihad to eradicate disparity. Rather, it is how their obsession with unmaking things to satisfy the greatest quantity destroys those qualities which make us unique and our lives valuable. We need to discover how to get more from our lives, not more into them, and that struggle is one which the West has been losing for a very long time, since perhaps the onset of the Enlightenment.

Considering how quickly information moves in our time, it's hard to imagine people taking the time to reflect when they're constantly being programmed to respond instantaneously. Speaking with the sincerity of an addict with a sizable social media account, it becomes very difficult to escape the cycle of constant gratification that emerges and step back to ask the harder questions. Most people don't, living instead at the edge of tension and in seeking to reduce such volatility, will instead conform and pick a safe path. The need for security, hardwired into the rodent portion of our cerebellum, finds satisfaction in these ways and the momentary respite needed for survival.

In a world quickly shifting beyond our comprehension, those who control stimulus have half the equation to manage people's behavior and therefore society. The other half comes from fear, from the animal reality of being which continues no matter where our minds may wander, and from those who would threaten it. Where the Internet offers hope, the world seems to only offer fear, and we still live now in the trauma of the greatest attack of our lives, the destruction of the World Trade Center which happened on September 11th, 2001.

Chapter 22: Perfecting the Unwinnable War: Terror as Enemy

9/11 marked the formal beginning of a paradigm shift. With the death of thousands of Americans, our people shifted away from the blasé indifference of the post Cold War period into the new anxious age where fear could come from any threat, but increasingly from non-state actors. An organization like Al Qaeda, small bands that are difficult to track, would become the new warriors and threat to civilization in the popular eye.

Many people believe that the truth of what happened on that day – and who was responsible – requires much more explanation that the official conclusions have drawn. Most infamously, the case of Building 7 has long troubled people. But whatever the precise means of destruction of the World Trade Center, the important question for us is how this seminal event has shifted the narrative.

People were afraid again. The images of death and suffering were etched into the mind's eye of several generations, and we demanded our government act. We wanted protection from the world. To ensure that the unthinkable would be prevented from happening again, a worthwhile but most likely futile endeavor, our deeply ironic national response was twofold: We granted even more expansive powers to the very people who had failed to prevent these attacks, and we went to war.

The Taliban was a brutal regime in Afghanistan for whom one needs feel no empathy, but as we are still in a low-grade war there 17 years later, it's worth asking what we have accomplished? The quick fall of the government masked a guerrilla war where the opposition blended back into the hills. Billions were spent to fight this battle, to destroy and rebuild, but beyond the instant gratification of taking down a hostile regime and replacing it with a corrupt one, it's hard to conclude the War on Terror was worth the price we paid.

Most painfully, our veterans who fought not just in Afghanistan, but also in the Second Gulf War in Iraq were expended in an opaque and ill-defined conflict. Lives and limbs were lost to insurgents, and civilians as warriors were forced to play peacekeepers and bring our foreign values to their strange lands. The universalists back in DC wanted to remake the Muslim world while making a few bucks on another lucrative contract in territories rich with energy. As a result, we now have a generation where many of our strongest and most patriotic are suffering from PTSD. They deserved better.

But leaving aside the foreign implications for a moment, the creation of the Department of Homeland Security was perhaps the most dangerous overreaction. We created an agency whose purpose was to track people in and outside the country, gave them as much money for weapons and training as they requested, and invited the government to legally embrace the surveillance abilities which the new digital platforms allowed them to consider.

The Patriot Act represented a collective cry of fear from the citizenry to do so something, but what it essentially accomplished was granting broad authority for our intelligence agencies to keep track of our own people. The new legislation enabled government to easily collect and obtain phone and e-mail conversations, bank records, credit card information, and monitor people on the suspicion of intent alone. This was a previously unprecedented assault upon the 4th Amendment provisions protecting us against unwarranted search and seizure.

In any time of panic, the social ethos makes an important shift which endures past the imminent threat: Whereas before 9/11, the primary mode of social interaction was respectful of privacy as the basic right of the citizen, fear shifted that mindset to something more akin to the assertion that those with nothing to hide should welcome scrutiny into their lives. See something, say something was branded into a whole generation, encouraging people to further increase their suspicion of each other, and in so doing, their alienation from each other.

The recurring theme became evident again: Government creates situations – in this case – the recurring involvement in the incredibly messy politics of the Middle East and Afghanistan – which led to these crises. The government stirred up trouble, often counting upon the very limited knowledge of the American population, and then acted falsely stunned when the meddling came back home in the form of radicalism and terror. But maybe, it's possible this chaos isn't just incompetence, but the creation of a means to justify the end of internal surveillance.

In the case of Afghanistan, it was well known the CIA intervened to help and train the people who would represent the core leadership of Al Qaeda as well as having had contact with the mujahideen of the Taliban during years of support in the 1980's. Bin Laden himself came from a prominent Saudi family whose ties with the West were so deep the school of Middle Eastern Studies at Oxford is named after them.

Years of searching failed to locate this mastermind who was reported dead years earlier and who was also supposedly undergoing dialysis. We never saw the body, and only when war support had flagged so far that a desperate President needed a PR boost, did we finally get our man. Conveniently, he was killed and disposed of without any evidence save for videos shared around the world.

I actually hate being so cynical, but after a lifetime where every war has been demonstrated to have a darker motive than the one promoted, where every new power granted to the government has been turned against the citizenry, and where the ideas put out in public run pretty much directly counter to the foundation of liberty and responsibility upon which we were founded, trust in what the government claims to have happened is not something I can take at face value.

One thing these numerous wars and police actions have done is set off mass migrations. People are moving on a scale rarely seen in human history, with the most incongruous example being here in the West. More so in Europe than America, we are now seeing people from the Islamic world coming in droves, bringing their ideology and cultural beliefs directly into conflict with the dominant secular paradigm. They make their own alliance where free reign is given to the new migrants to enforce their dogma, a useful weapon which keeps the majority silent.

To be the majority today is to live in fear of crime from people who come from cultures where violence is a daily occurrence, while also in shame from the rebuke of not being tolerant enough. Starting with Bush 43's false praise and acclamation of the virtues of Islam, our nations have gone out of their way to rationalize this religion as something completely opposite from what it truly promotes.

Islam is not a religion of peace, but rather a movement that demands submission. It spreads like a war band, forcing conversions by the knife and holding people the same way. It treats women as chattel, embraces child marriage, and has no separation of state from the church. Jihad is the universal duty of Muslims, using Taqiyya, a form of strategic falsehood, to find position and success. It is a political ideology of control through forcing people to submit – a religion loved by the Marxist mindset that believes in absolute equality.

Saying such things in polite society will get you exiled. Not believing such things and living in contravention of them might get you killed, however. We see story after story of what the migrants bring to the table, and don't even consider the cost of the money we're spending to replace the native people of our lands and countries with these foreigners. Our governments stopped serving us, and instead served their own cause by inviting the foxes into the hen house.

But that's why this struggle is also so hard. We've been asking why no one has ever been able to organize in order to stop the descent into insanity. And it's easy to see that while culture has been degraded, and the government has become a behemoth, that the people of good character needed for such a fight have always been distracted into fighting another battle. Ironically, it was usually those battles which failed to accomplish the good goal of preserving our civilization, but always left the government in a more powerful position afterward.

We called these days conservative, sometimes masquerading as the deliberate obfuscation of neoconservatism, but they weren't. Limited government with the promised humbler foreign policy never materialized. We got new wars and new toys, but we never found security. Americans are never permitted that outcome, which might just be obtainable if we decided not to play global hegemon in defense of the neoliberal world order, where our men bleed to ensure global elites can retain their positions. Try speaking against that and see how the term isolationist is used to paint someone rational as a coward by the right, and a bigot by the left.

But the reason we can't defeat terror, besides the obvious reality that terrorism is a tactic and not an ideology, is because we don't call things what they are. We should be unrepentant in casting aspersions against Islam, and in not welcoming people into our countries whose faith is incompatible with our own. We shouldn't need a surveillance state to watch these people because there is no reason to invite them in, save for the same virtue signaling stupidity that amounts to pathological altruism.

It's weird how we would invite our enemy into our midst. It's insane that people went for this, but this is what happens when fear and trauma short-circuit logic. When truly momentous events happen, the paradigm shifts entirely, but it just never seems to work to get us where we want to be. Such disappointment is as true for those who just want the threat to subside as for those of us who instead want a return to beliefs that made more sense.

But that wasn't what happened after the 9/11 attacks. We asked our government to become the perfect spies, and they gladly took the resources and responsibility to seek high and low. Is it any surprise given these powers, that they would ultimately use them just as much to spy on our own American people as any foreign threats? After all, terror could lurk anywhere, and the all too familiar never again refrain was used once more to quiet Americans from legitimate inquiry.

A new agenda on a global scale was being pushed once more, and this time, the fears being pushed would be far larger and more demanding. The world itself was at risk, not just from violence of people, but from our very society itself. And unsurprisingly, the governments had come up with solutions to share to this crisis centered around Global Warming. Because even in a time where there was no military threat, there always must be a crisis at hand.

Chapter 23: A Once Cool Idea Gets Hot: Fabricating a Global Cause

Fear has a funny way of making people see everything as a problem and every condition as a threat. Once those hardwired instincts kick in, then the part of our brains that reasons shuts down, and we act to make problems go away. The bigger the threat, the more quickly we want it addressed, and the less critical we will be of proposed solutions. Keep this state of mind in consideration, bolstered by an amorphous War on Terror, as the newest global threat was presented: Climate Change.

The idea that industrial economies can reshape the environment is not new. One can go back to Victorian England with its many smoking cauldrons pumping soot into the sky and people were proclaiming even then that our environment would be forever lost and beyond repair. But in the modern era, the panic about changing climates actually began in the 1970's with forecasts of global cooling which would lead to mass starvation.

When that didn't happen, global warming became the big scare in the 1990's and beyond, with multiple pleas to save the ozone layer and an effort against CFCs found in various aerosol products. Whether the threat was overstated, or the public awareness campaign worked, we rarely hear about the ozone crisis anymore, so I can only assume it was fixed. But global warming has continued to be used to provoke fears of the polar ice caps melting, raising the seas to drown coastal cities.

Now, that hasn't happened yet. As it turns out, weather remains sporadic and highly regionalized, more responsive to the cycles of the sun than anything we do here on Earth – absent some known phenomena such as the contribution to global cooling made by volcanic eruptions. Much money has been set aside for research to prove climate change theories, and unsurprisingly, the evidence has been produced to fit the theory, which is the pathway to power and prestige for an academic.

Of course, the numerous stories and scandals revealing falsification of evidence are called outliers. And with good reason, because if you want to build a global governance structure around a single culture, you need a threat which impacts everyone to organize people together. Climate change, the latest iteration of a threat to not just humanity, but the plants and animals which we tend to love even more because they don't have the unpleasant habit of voicing dissenting opinions, is the perfect feel-good cause to marshal support.

Therefore, groups like the United Nations, bolstered by an army of progressive think tanks, love to form commissions promoting ideas like sustainable living under the infamous artifice called Agenda 21. A more radical social programming agenda to try to homogenize humanity and reduce our capabilities has never been pushed by the institutional class, looking to control what people eat, what they grow, their ability to reproduce, and of course, the governments of the world.

Industry is to be slowed and opportunity limited to sustainable levels. Governments will replace those options with a level of support all can enjoy, and we can realize the dream of Fukuyama and Marx alike: An end to history in a promised paradise. A green friendly Earth where all cultures and nations exist in harmony sounds great, but it has a very high cost.

Cap and trade and carbon credits were all the buzz just a few years ago. The basic theory was the world could only afford to produce so much carbon dioxide (CO_2) so the bureaucrats decided to divide up who could produce what according to population and poverty. Never ones to miss the opportunity to redistribute assets from the wealthy to the poor, their plan called for paralyzing the economies of the West, of America and Europe most specifically, to realize their dream. Of course, if western companies wanted to continue producing their goods, they could do so but only if they shifted their operations to Third World countries where their carbon exhaust output still had some capacity according to these arbitrarily chosen levels. Or, they could bribe these countries to buy a share, realizing the social justice of elevating the poor.

Such thinking could only cost American jobs, siphon away American wealth, and make areas whose values and thinking is often the opposite of ours stronger. But that is the logic of globalism 2.0: Force everyone together into one group by whatever means necessary, and watch the differences resolve themselves. The poor might be slightly better off, the wealthy countries will be brought down somewhat, and so long as the elites control policy, the march toward equality – now the only sustainable solution – marches on.

If you question the intent of this climate change agenda, you will feel all the fury hot air can muster. When one notes that many of us learned in science classes years ago that the production of additional carbon dioxide would serve as fuel for plants, something we've observed as Earth has never been greener, people with many initials after their name call such basic reasoning preposterous.   Who are we, whose only knowledge is general and who dare to consider ourselves thinkers, to question so-called settled science?

If you were to ask if science represents theories and hypothesis that require constant re-examination, a process to understand the world by constantly trying and discarding old ideas in favor of new ideas that fit the data of reality better, you would only receive a stammering retort that "everyone knows certain things are true." Pure dogma. While I agree this holds true about certain hardwired instincts, such a claim does not hold for environmentalism in our age, where we see professors working a little too hard to defend something they want to be true because if they were to debunk it, they would lose their funding.

Understanding entirely why people would trust professors above the amoral corporations who will collect and sell energy at any price, green energy is an interesting alternative. But it doesn't work economically at present for our needs, and while research into any alternate mode of producing energy seems intelligent, doesn't it seem like government subsidy has reached the point of being a handout? I wonder how many other companies like Solyndra were out there? So many of these companies represent nice ideas that don't work very well in practice and which only exist due to government support: A Marxist approach to energy.

Having worked in government, I saw firsthand how not just municipalities, but businesses would rush to embrace the new dogma, greased by refunds and tax credits, and changing the culture toward sustainability through the thousand totems out there to reflect the consensus that we must live differently. While I'm all for being responsible stewards, it doesn't take much imagination to see how this philosophy is designed to limit our means of expression.

We are encouraged to be part of the hive. What we want individually does not matter, but instead we must think only of the greater good. We must give up the right to own more, because others lack. We must give up our cherished ideas of right and wrong, so we can come together to tackle problems bigger than ourselves. Less is more, because each owns all.

Writing such Marxist drivel pains me, but that's the essential argument the institutional elites are making once more, even as they live quite differently in their own jet-setter lives, this time using the fear of an external threat to encourage us to not ask questions and just put our heads down to battle against climate change. While there are good and well-intended people fighting for our planet who should not be impugned for their idealism, there's ample and immediately apparent evidence that the climate change dogma isn't just about limiting our waste.

If the goal were truly to encourage living within our environmental means, why is it that every government, bank, and international institution rushed to bailout the very people encouraging such waste? Could it be because the capitalists and communists ended up yet again on the same side? They exist as enemies in the public sphere, but neither removes the other, because it is their ostentatious struggle that is used to induce us to surrender our rights and our nations.

Chapter 24: When Food Becomes Junk

For all the talk given about the environment and how important it is to both national and international personalities, there has never been more of a push to remove people from what is healthy for them. We can start with something as basic as our food supply and our farms, a once diversified selection driven by family-run businesses and now increasingly organized into corporate profit centers. Consumption has replaced nutrition as a core value, and the economics of scale have been used to push people who once enjoyed the country life toward the city, whether they want it or not, because that's another vector for control.

If you are fortunate enough to either live in the country or to have a local farmer's market where you can purchase fruits, vegetables, or meats, and can bring them directly to the plate, the amazing thing is how different they taste, how vibrant they are, and after years of eating this way, how much clearer one's mind and health become from enjoying real food. By contrast, if you only get your food from some supercenter where meat seems to grow off cellophane, no matter how nice the choices often look, something is clearly missing.

You would think a government concerned for the welfare of its citizens would encourage local access to food as both a means to better public health as well as meeting food security issues. I would give credit to a few innovative programs through the USDA which provide help, but these go against the main thrust where instead of helping farms and farmers, we see a cynical movement against those who provide food and to restrict the most basic of needs.

Any such discussion which doesn't feature Monsanto prominently is derelict. The studies on how terrible Roundup is for animal and human health are numerous, and yet the turnstile between the USDA, FDA, and corporations like this has been continuing for many years, picking up speed through the 1990's in the post-NAFTA period. Brilliant innovations like the terminator gene designed to create food dependency, as well as farmer obligation, are used to pollute the seed bank of the nation to realize higher yield for one season at the potential expense of the very viability of a national food crop. This insanity would be stopped by any sane government before it could evolve into a disaster through cross-pollination, but instead, farmers were sued out of business for involuntary infringement of patent law because pollen from a corn variety they aren't even growing drifted into their field on the wind and polluted their seed crop.

If that seems too extreme, consider the much more discussed topic of genetically modified organisms (GMOs). I can only imagine what combinations have been put into production at this point, but I recall vividly the first mix that really drew attention in a major way was when fish genes were spliced into tomatoes to ensure greater longevity.

While I understand tomatoes can be tender and won't keep forever, it's amazing how we change the tomato itself into some freakish hybrid to accommodate logistics needs of global corporations, trusting there will be no ill side-effects.

Whether or not my caution represents the backward thinking of a Luddite is debatable, but a great many nations around the world share the same concerns. Much of Europe, Russia, and Asia reject much of American agriculture specifically because of our lax standards relating to GMO contamination, especially prominent in staple crops like corn, wheat, and soy just to name a few. Worse still, since these represent the feed stock for most poultry, pork, and beef that we consume, any issues these crops pass along comes to us just as easily through protein.

Another example of how public health is compromised is how antibiotics have been used for years in meat and milk production. Instead of focusing on how pervasive antibiotic use for rapid weight gain or as a disease preventative in healthy animals might adversely affect human or animal health, or even play an important role in creating antibiotic resistant diseases, optimizing for profit motive and pushing product has become the priority of our regulatory agencies. This trend is by no means restricted to food, but more likely the inevitable outcome of the confluence of money, government, and business. Unless someone can afford to pay the considerable premium for grass-fed beef and organic milk, and unless they happened to do the research to determine that these products are better, how would anyone know the dangers of their own consumption when agencies are so clearly compromised?

If you think about it, given such cavalier attitudes about our food supply, it's no accident so many people are unwell. Wheat and flour were the foundational blocks of western civilization. Now gluten is one of the fastest growing sensitivities where even touching certain wheat-based products makes many people sick. Could it possibly be because when the wheat was spliced with some other genetic blend, or potentially inserted into another unrelated item, the body was taught to reject what had once sustained millions of people with little trouble?

As I write this, I think of the dismal school lunches that have come into being, looking so tiny and unappetizing that many students stopped eating them. How are young minds supposed to ask questions and understand the world without adequate nutrition? Even though the subsidized school lunch program covered up for the inadequacy of many parents in fulfilling a basic function, it was a real success despite its costs. This program has slid into decay because of ever- evolving and worsening standards which hurt the children most in the end. Instead of learning to think, they only have enough energy to follow.

Whether one is provided subsidy for food or spends their own money, it seems we all end up in that same dilemma in that eating affordably means eating unwell. I've always referred to this as "the ketchup paradox," where the cost of a processed item in ketchup is less than the cost of purchasing tomatoes to make it. Eating healthy presents a huge challenge for us all and beyond preventing an outbreak of infection that draws public ire, we don't see the commitment to eat well in America.

Beyond the obvious profit motive, our diets which are calorie rich and infused with bad items like high fructose corn syrup render us less potent. We can sustain ourselves, but we don't function optimally. We have an array of sugars that can be incredibly tasty but also addicting, no less so than any other drug of choice. In truth, what sugar does to the body is more addicting in many ways than many prohibited substances and diabetes no less awful a fate, but these risks are deemed acceptable and even useful because they help keep the citizens pacified. A mouth stuffed with potato chips won't complain past the couch.

One can argue this is a lifestyle choice to which people should be held to account. I heartily agree and think we should call people out on poor choices, saying this as a person who made many poor choices growing up and has learned a better way. Yet, the path to live differently is filled with many artificial obstacles, something you learn quickly if you happen to reside in the country. Watch people get sent to jail for consuming raw milk and you wonder how a state that can't find a person who overstays a visa can glibly attack someone for choosing to eat a natural food.

Try using herbal medicines and see how quickly the FDA, acting as the attack dog for the Big Pharma profit engine, comes down upon you. It should be the most basic thing in the world to recognize that vitamins and minerals can be incredibly healthy, and to remember many standard medicines come from the natural world rather than chemical engineering. But the war on health seeks to constrain and limit our choices to be healthy, in some cases criminalizing options which work well for people in the ubiquitous assertion the state knows best. How can we ever doubt that?

Whole books have been written about the litany of items dumped in our environment. Whether it is fluoride and estrogen in the water, aluminum strewn in waffling lines across the sky, or any of a host of other items purportedly either for our health or at least supposedly neutral to the natural requirements of our bodies, there are few places we can go where we haven't changed things. Rural areas are usually somewhat less impacted, but even out here in the sticks, one sees these things and cannot help but wonder what we are doing to ourselves. We cannot trust a government who looks only at the ledger, and who sees themselves driven more by ideas than regard for the people themselves, a disconnect which has sadly been demonstrated through all the observations of this and many other volumes.

As the farms started to shutter and the gas prices fluctuated more, the government has done everything it can not just to attack food and wellness, but to encourage people away from rural life. Policies are designed to bring people near the city, so they can live where their needs can be more easily met by providers and services, but the cost of such convenience is to sacrifice our own self-sufficiency as a nation and closeness to nature which truly sustains us. I do not think we even begin to understand what this involuntary choice means, but let's cast the question into a bigger picture.

Since the dawn of human history, man has lived in balance with the land, having respect for it not because of some campaign, but because of the personal and intimate realization that the land sustains us. Food, water, shelter, and all goods, no matter how refined, ultimately come from the Earth. Living that reality creates a degree of environment awareness no city can ever equal, and a respect for life, death, health, sickness, family, and community as a cycle of life. And we have lost that, and our state does everything it can to draw us further away from that natural connection, and closer to big cities as if in a hive.

Our programmed future is disconnected and atomized from the Earth, but bound together in a hive of commerce, of technology, and in clusters of incredible density. How does living like a bee or an ant change who we are? Will we care less for one another when we live literally one floor above another in a sea of humanity? Can anyone care the same way when such masses of people make us all anonymous? Is that truly liberation? Or is it the loss of self? Most people don't even have the context to ask these questions and consider what has potentially been lost. For if we have a nature, whatever it is, surely millennia of history show this is not it.

Unfortunately, agriculture is now a business and just like any other business, it has become larger and less accountable. The only good thing I can say is at least it is somewhat constrained by the choices of the consumer, which even when made poorly, require a minimal degree of concern if only to retain market share. For our bigger sectors like energy and banking, this may no longer be the case, as can be amply demonstrated by just how far the government has gone to assure the health of the banks – in sad juxtaposition to how indifferent it seems about the health of the people.

Chapter 25: Their Loans, Your Taxes. How We Subsidize Finance

No one wanted the bailout of Wall Street in 2008. People who usually vote Democrat were marching in the streets with their Occupy Wall Street chants, rightly questioning corporate greed. People who usually vote Republican were saying that no business should be treated as too big to fail, pointing out the moral peril of subsidizing failure, an equally valid and fervent case against bailing out the banks. A Presidential election was in the balance as this crisis spiraled out of control, but members of both parties and both candidates came together to do what they do best: To screw the people and save the elites over the regular folk.

The losses racked up by the banks and various insurance entities due to reckless spending and gambling were covered by the government, who freely appropriated tax payer money to save the rich, further impoverishing the poor and middle classes. The people who made billions, who had been creating paper wealth through interest and clever fictions, found themselves saved and encouraged to begin anew without any sanction. More proof banks have owned America since at least 1913.

Whoever owns the banks can buy the culture. Our government protects the banks from the people, and the people who own the banks put the ideas out there that ensure the government keeps paying for their ideas.

Couched in the clever language of universal equality, the result is almost always a reduction in the liberties, assets, or opportunities of the average citizen. A few elites benefit, and we all pay their costs.

The way this scam worked is as follows. During the 1990's, the policymakers decided that it would be beneficial if everyone owned a house. There were many people whose credit or other factors precluded their financial trustworthiness to acquire a home loan. To enable these purchases to happen, the government had to change lending guidelines to get money into the market, which they did through Fannie Mae (FNMA – Federal National Mortgage Association) and Freddie Mac, a similar lending entity. The government agreed to provide the insurance and collateral so people who could not afford to purchase homes through conventional means could obtain them.

Predictably, the decision to open lending coupled with government support, caused a spike in home prices and in building new homes. The policy makers saw this as a net positive because it caused economic growth while also giving people a sense of ownership, but all this was done upon the presumption and basic requirement that the value of homes would continue rising indefinitely and the default interest rate would stay above a certain level.

The same problem currently exists with the student loan market. Where colleges used to be affordable, the government working to mandate access to college for everyone has caused the price of college to rise at multiples of the rate of inflation, yet since borrowers are forced to repay student loans without any option of default, the loans remain incredibly attractive to lenders who know students can't use bankruptcy or any other form of relief to escape a poorly made decision. Colleges, through using professors to preach the importance of caring for the poor, implement pretty much the opposite philosophy through their administration. Colleges have never been flusher with cash as they raise tuition regularly, knowing the government will pick up the tab with guaranteed loans. Watch for this bubble to burst next, much how the housing one went.

What really exacerbated the problem were two interrelated trends. First, because nothing had traditionally been seen in the private market as being a more secure investment than mortgages, there was a great deal of capital out there waiting to be invested. But, the biggest sources of financial investment out there have been big institutional funds, conservative in their fiscal priorities, and looking for a guaranteed rate of return with minimal risk.

Mortgages fit the bill, but individually, there was no way these mortgages would suffice. For simplicity, let's say each had a 75% likelihood of being fulfilled, based upon the reasonable supposition that even people of modest means would want to keep the roof over their heads. While one mortgage like this might represent a rather chancy investment, akin to junk bonds which are high risk/high reward opportunities, combining a bundle of these mortgages together changed the math on the books. A person owning just 5 of these mortgages would see the mathematical probability that 98% would offer a return on investment, and they were bundled in lots of hundreds or thousands before they were placed for sale. They looked secure.

So long as the market kept rising, the mortgages always retained and gained value. In places like Florida, Arizona, and California, homes were being built just as quickly as possible, as there seemed to be a limitless number of buyers wanting to sink their money into real estate. The decades long trend of rising home prices seemed to make these investments easy money, so homes were purchased as often by speculators as actual prospective home owners ... until the credit started to crunch and properties available so outpaced the demand that homes weren't moving any more. Property values began to retreat.

A house which had been worth $300,000 one year quickly slid to be worth only $150,000 the next, and the high-risk property owners who had purchased their residence upon the presumption their asset would appreciate suddenly found themselves upside down. They owed more on their houses than the actual market value and having only put down limited money or no money at all, loans which naturally arose out of the free lending environment social policy encouraged, people made the economic decision to walk away from these debts in many cases.

At the same time, investors owning multiple properties also panicked and tried to sell out of their positions. As with any other panic, once it begins, it is hard to stop the money from flowing away from the cause of the disturbance. And in this case, the disturbance threatened to catch many banks and insurance companies. While the banks who held such mortgages were exposed, they at least had the collateral of the properties themselves.

Well-deserving of its own deep independent examination, banks have a time-honored tradition of collateralization, whereby they offer loans to desperate people, knowing they are unlikely to be paid back, and using this method to convert their loans into tangible assets. One outcome of the bailout was that the loans banks were legally permitted to offer from fractional reserve banking were transformed into real assets of tangible value when the properties were foreclosed upon during the crisis.

But because they could at least re-sell or rent out the properties, they were not the most exposed actors. Worse still were companies like Bear Stearns which collapsed and AIG which was rescued. These companies operated in a world of derivatives. High finance plays many games so people can bet money different ways. As a gambler understands, the house always wins because they collect the vig, a fee from the players, and so too does Wall Street. They allow certain investors to bet on whether a given stock or fund will fail.

The despicable part of the bailout is what happened with companies such as AIG. AIG issued insurance to protect investors against homeowners defaulting on their loans, while at the same time standing to gain via shorting the derivatives market if those loans were to fail. This is a terrible conflict of interest, and the worst example in some time of how a company could protect itself by screwing over its own customers. The whole market seemed to be in a similar position because greed and overconfidence had led them to bet on perpetual growth. When it failed, the entire economy was put at risk.

For the individual investor unfamiliar with the magic that happens in lower Manhattan, the result would have been destroyed 401K portfolios, meaning the promised happy retirement for the average citizen would quickly become a delusion. The private banks would collapse and the people who were unwitting bettors would be outraged. So, the central banks stepped in, and floated many billions in liquidity to swallow these mistakes.

Just how the Fed did this remains concealed, but those snippets revealed demonstrate many billions of dollars were loaned to foreign entities to cover their exposure. Money was printed at a rapid clip and used to buy these bundled mortgages, called quantitative easing, to ensure credit did not stop flowing. Even though such action inherently made our fiat currency even less valuable, the storm was weathered with the system intact after the government promised to bailout the bankers.

AIG was granted the free money, but homeowners with mortgages collateralized with property worth less than the loans were out of luck. There were government finance programs to reduce the interest rate for people at the lowest end of the income scale, but even at that, who would want to stay in houses now worth half the mortgage owed on them? Many homeowners still haven't recovered from the fiasco of buying houses at artificially inflated prices, and even a decade later are still "upside down" on their mortgages, while the banks are free and clear. The beneficiaries of the bailout have made clear that both of our political parties weren't looking out for the little guy.

This chapter is highly technical by the standards of this volume, but it's important because beneath all the juicy details, the scam remains the same. Those without are pitted against one another, promised equality and better opportunity, but in reality, we get left holding the proverbial bag and those with power and access further expand their hegemony. They take away our money as well as our values, and even when we rise to ask for something different, rarely do we get more than empty rhetoric in reply.

Chapter 26: Obama and the Great White Hope: The Post-Racial Lie

Hope and change is what we were promised. We were told about a lot of hopes, but when Obama left the White House, we had only pocket change remaining. In many ways, his Presidency represented the epitome of the triumph of progressive rhetoric over physical reality, with predictable results.

Obama was elected because the Republicans were stupid and complicit enough to put a candidate against him whose contributions to limited government were to advocate for endless wars on unwinnable terms, and who rushed to be seen supporting the bankers. So, people decided to vote for the unknown quantity who spoke well, used marketing so vague it could appeal to anyone, and played into the national fantasy that race is an unpleasant fiction of the past.

White liberals who voted for a black guy so they could feel a sense of absolution from artificially created white guilt, long teased by the Establishment, and a culture which has actively encouraged self-hatred in the majority – both on the racial and cultural level, combined to give Obama an overwhelming mandate. The goal was to demonstrate how far we had come, so a junior Senator in his first term with a very sparse voting record was presented as a messianic figure for America to embrace.

I can understand why black people were proud to see Obama elected as one of their own. But looking back after eight years of that experience, he didn't really help make things better for either the minorities or the majority. He took care of the banks who helped get him elected and went on an international apology tour where we took our money and tried to buy the forgiveness of everyone and anyone who would accept it. He supported racial actions, but in a way that only exacerbated anger and frustration.

Consider Black Lives Matter. This group – which was responsible for the assassination of police officers in Dallas, Texas – was protected by the Justice Department when Eric Holder was in office. Instead of promoting law and order, this regime pushed for community policing guidelines designed to essentially put certain groups above and beyond the law. Just ask Loretta Lynch when she isn't busy aboard some airplane what deals were really made.

Promises were made of a better economy and opportunity, but the shovel-ready jobs promised for our people went straight to the grave. But one could not speak too loudly or angrily about these failures, because our President said all the right things about working together, and to criticize him would be racist and the worst expression of white privilege. Legitimate discourse was marginalized, and the media fawned predictably for eight years of slow, sullen mediocrity.

The gates remained open as America, along with Europe, became lands of opportunity save for those who were born here, and in this, all races are included. Our children were educated in a system where they were taught in such a way that they learned to follow orders rather than ask questions., Schools twisted knowledge itself into something incomprehensible, as is the case with Common Core, a government mandated curriculum which replaced mathematics with estimation and facts with more pleasant fictions.

Evidently, we are supposed to neither think nor count. Our children, especially those from impoverished areas, are struggling to compete, but instead of improving the quality of education, our government's answer is to import foreigners. The lives are made harder for those who are here and who were born here, as if we have no right to place the interests of our own people – by any terms – above the good of this emergent globalized system. We are enlightened, but it turns out when everyone gets to that point, all we have are a bunch of dimwits.

But Obama was the fulfillment of the cultural Marxist strategy, a platform devoid of content save to realize the long-term goal of equality for all people. Mobilizing race as the means to get elected, he maximized the black vote based on pure identity, and managed to get re-elected despite having few accomplishments to his name. Frankly, he would have likely been elected to a third term were he permitted to run, because we've reached the point where identity is how people vote.

Blacks vote Democrat. Latinos vote Democrat. Only whites divide their votes, because we're the only ones who don't think of our own people when we vote. This is because fifty years of culture and education have taught us to hate who we are, and to see ourselves as some sort of oppressors rather than as the originators of the civilization which powers most of the world at this point. We are only allowed to exist politically in absence, a gap which everyone sees as central to American society, but which we are not allowed to comment upon or work with, save as a negative to erase the core of who we are as a people.

Some call this white genocide. At a minimum, it is white displacement. It starts by negating our proud legacy as a people, taking away the accomplishments of our civilization. It accelerates with an agenda to bring in people by the hundreds of thousands into only countries founded by white people. It is facilitated by a media that puts out imagery daily encouraging our submission and marginalization. And it ends, as it does now in South Africa, with the loss of our rights and status as we become minorities.

And we will not be minorities in a beneficent country where equality is the goal either. We merely have to look beneath that lip service to see how aggressively all the factions of the left speak against our majority. Our academics literally call whiteness a crime against humanity. Wherever the left holds power, white cops have been sent to jail for apprehending black criminals in the act of violent crime. We are told that our guns are the real threat, that our church is the force of evil, and that our people do not warrant having their grievances considered, for we are made responsible for all of society's ills.

It would be entirely correct to say that leftists did it to themselves. Could it be that instead of blaming whitey, they should point instead to years of radicalizing people against success and shattering our culture into a thousand pieces? Could having music and television that glorify sex and violence while seeking to destroy the family have made people into less than they once were? Could giving people free money instead of teaching them how to provide for themselves, reduce their dignity and virtue?

Could it be that the success of western civilization was no accident at all, but rather the result of a tremendous effort led by a group of people who came out of Europe and into this country with a certain set of ideals, driven by hard work and the desire to live virtuously, and in fact that all our successes to this very day originate from that core of people? Can you say the success of our civilization was driven by such people, supplemented by those who shared their core ideas, rather than this unsustainable idea that welfare for everyone will lead to happiness?

No, you can't say that. Because that's racist.

It's racist to say that unequal outcomes might be the result of races being different. It's sexist to say men and women aren't the same, and that maybe the difference between masculine and feminine is not purely arbitrary. It's prejudiced to say one faith which emphasizes service and sacrifice might work better than one which converts by the sword, but could it just be possible our shared convictions gave us strength and character?

We are taught to feel shame about who we are by this coalition of the ascendant, and somehow convinced to feel despair about who we have been and what we have done. Mistakes were made, but in the annals of history, there has rarely been a gentler and more just civilization than the one we built together, and whose fundamental decency endures today, despite the pages of provocation already shared.

But these ideas themselves are under threat and under attack. Because the end game for the Marxists, progressives, leftists, and all their allies has always been about control. To realize equality, they must unmake all things of quality, and it is no accident they have long centered their attack on white America, a group bigger than just race, of people who believe traditional values and who honor our traditions and our families. They would have us believe we are the reason so many fail, even as they know the only reason they endure is at our charity and our sufferance.

We showed that in 2016 by electing Donald Trump. Both the majority and those in the minority who realized the charlatan song of the left was offering no solutions came together against the media, the academics, the political establishment, and the banks to offer a stinging rebuke. We began the last stand for our culture, but the question now is what we do with this fight?

This is what I was thinking when I stood up and looked into those hateful cameras trying to bend me into submission. We have all given enough, and instead, isn't it time we take back what is ours? They took my job, and perhaps they took my name, but they didn't take away my beliefs or my legacy, and I think we still have that fight within.

Chapter 27: Know that History is Always Fabricated

Odds are pretty good you won't be hearing about this version of history in schools or on the television, but I encourage anyone reading this book to do your own research and draw your own conclusions about what is true. We don't need more people just following along because someone better educated says so – we need intelligent and active citizens who learn things on their own.

I purposely neglected to chase down citations for two reasons. First, having a bunch of other people echoing what one repeats only shows the strength of institutional support and not the inherent value or truthfulness of an idea. But second, you really need to take some time to understand, as your world view may shift radically as you expose yourself to suppressed ideas, facts, and concepts.

History is not what you have been told. It is complicated, contradictory, and constantly under revision. In the last twenty-five years especially, much of what was once held to be sacred has been erased and is being replaced with a false and radical agenda-driven narrative. The people who control our society, from the government to the colleges and on to the media, have worked long to mold us into something less than we once were. Whether they do so for peace or submission, the question this book begs you to consider is if this is what you want.

Speaking only for myself, I cannot abide the thought that we must give up our opportunity to achieve more, to be a people united by one culture in pursuit of common goals. Because only with that sort of culture would it be possible to heal some of the widest divides in this country. I say this as an unabashed race realist, knowing that only when we root all our relations, both social and individual, in fact, can we ever achieve mutual amity and the understanding where we don't suspect one another.

My parents taught me to be honest, and to the very best of my ability, and not without a degree of fear for consequences that will accrue, I've written this understanding. My hope is that it will serve as a beacon for others in their own search and will help those out there to understand both my own efforts and those of many others who are branded as evil and wicked by the lying media.

We love our people. We love our race. We love our culture. We love our civilization. And without hatred of anyone for who they are, we seek to recover what was lost. We want families again where men and women both have dignity and where life matters more than money. We expect responsibility but with opportunity also for achievement, instead of a low ceiling underneath which we are all supposed to squat.

Most importantly, we choose quality over quantity. That is the rallying cry, that we embrace competition because we can do better, we can be better, and we have the courage to call out right from wrong, good from evil, and get past this cancerous relativism. Any thinking person can do so, and all people of good character will be allies in the culture war that is brewing.

As I write, marches have become more common and the sides are radicalizing. Having failed to secure power through elections, leftists march in the streets threatening to take away the guns which have limited their agenda from implementation. Their allies in corporate media censor voices of dissent under community guidelines, and work to boycott us from having financial existence, let along parity. War is coming – whether we wish it or not – as their resistance pledges.

Yet, we remain because we have reason, passion, and true justice on our side. We are the thinkers who can create and laugh. We are the fighters who believe in people and identity, seeing culture not as interchangeable, but as unique and worthy of preservation. Lastly, we are fighting to create, whereas they are only offering to destroy more of what we are. I think we've given away enough.

Whether you agree or not is your decision, but if you take nothing else from this book, please remember to exercise a healthy suspicion of whatever anyone tells you. The one immutable truth is that people involved in politics and culture always have their own agendas, and many will lie to you and use your own best instincts and impulses against you. This has been done time and time again to the

American people, and one wonders how we can survive much longer if this trend is permitted to continue.

It's up to each of us to decide if that is the case. You now know why I'm standing up, and I thank everyone who listened and hope those of us who ask how so much has been lost will soon be standing together to reclaim what has ever been ours: Our manifest destiny.

Conclusion: First Steps Toward Reclaiming Our Country

For those who agree with this reading, I'll answer the obvious question and say I don't know how we fix this. What happened...really, what was done to our country was the work of generations of effort and there will be no quick or easy fix. It will take much pain, effort, and exertion to rediscover what was lost and to build new solutions to our current problems.

I think it starts with courage. People need to be able to say what they believe without fear of judgment and consequence. Nothing I said was so extreme as to warrant the response I received, which is how I knew I had touched upon an agenda being enforced upon our people. I understood from the moment the first story broke that I would be set up to be an example, and so I try to take that responsibility seriously by showing how someone can speak on difficult issues with decency, good humor and honesty.

My project for which I was so widely derided aimed to bring people together as people and beyond politics. We were a cultural movement who wanted to see things more localized, more self-sufficient, and rooted in families. It was a very optimistic and hopeful vision, and I think that's why it was attacked so vehemently. The left will not just let us have a better tomorrow – they will destroy us one by one unless we work together.

I also know from a lifetime in politics that the struggle will be very hard. Those of us used to living as individuals, exercising reason and protecting our families, are not so practiced in coming together in mutual support. We assume taking care of our own immediate family is enough, but that no longer remains true. When huge portions of people are being radicalized against you on the premise you stole what they once had and delivered to you, the old conservative method of individual achievement isn't going to work – and it hasn't for many years.

As I complete this book, I have begun working on new project I call the National Right (www.nationalright.us) which is rooted in one key idea and four key values which might unite us. If they offer resistance, let us instead offer a renaissance. They offer anger and destruction, let us offer creation and hope.

The central idea I support is we should build our life around quality rather than equality. We've been trapped in this false paradigm that we must either take care of the most people or have the most stuff to be happy. Both reinforce one another and neither takes account of the true happiness most people experience in their lives, in either the human connection to one another or the calling to a higher power such as I find in my Christian faith.

Ask each day how to live a better life and live unafraid to call out those who offer something which will make your life worse. This gets harder when we deal with the distasteful reality that this sometimes means telling certain people they are not welcome. But until we learn to close our doors against those things which will hurt us, how can we protect and defend our own? We may call out to those who would listen, but to give ourselves over to those who think the opposite of us is a surrender which we can no longer afford. Four key principles apply:

Responsibility – Take charge of your own life and actions, showing courage balanced by temperament.

Liberty – You are responsible for your actions, and what you do will preserve what options you leave available for not just yourself, but all around you.

Morality – Different ideas are of different value and it is incumbent upon each of us to strive to seek out that which is better.

Identity – When we find where we belong, comfort and pride in who we are, only then can we work together to achieve our aspirations and realize our combined strength.

These sound very simple, as most useful ideas are, but each is a rebuke to the dominant cultural ideal. We are told we are not responsible for our lives, but rather exist to blame others, fostering a culture of resentment and the hatred and violence which follow. Such inequity is used to justify surrender of our liberties to an ever-growing authority working against us. Morality itself is attacked to remove the authority of anything that might counter the singular idea promoted by culture and the state. Lastly, when it comes to identity, those groups who work to push toward the lowest common denominator are empowered, but those of us seeking to preserve what built our civilization are targeted for destruction.

I know identity is the hardest point for most people of good character because we have been raised not to think collectively and to think of people solely as individuals. I would never dream or suggest people think otherwise in how they relate to others, but we must also realize that when we cede the ability to speak of ourselves as a group, to ensure we have the same regard and interest given to our concerns, that we essentially become boxed out from the discussion by those who take their group identity for granted. That has happened for decades on the left, and that's why our multicultural society has devolved into racial strife, larger inequity, and the real possibility of prolonged conflict.

For white people, when we embrace our own identity once more as a source of pride, that will put an end to the facile arguments that prevent us from speaking out against bad ideas because the specter of racism is held over our heads as a threat. We are the ones who enforce this most dangerous of stigmas, internalizing such guilt as we are taught, and I would argue without any reason. We can love our own without hating the other, and if we do that, it might be a much better lesson than what we can observe is being taught by our adversaries.

For all people who aren't white, please know that this movement that is rising is not motivated by hatred for you, for the truth is we respect how you show pride in your people and your achievements and wish only to claim the same equal ground for ourselves. Only when we meet on the same field can we begin to find genuine regard, respect, and mutual understanding.

These are difficult things to discuss and think about, but these conversations need to begin, and we need to support one another in a new search. My hope is that a renaissance may truly emerge where we start asking again how we can live better instead of only how we can feed more mouths. We should ask what we want from life, not how much stuff will satisfy our wants.

This begins when we start asking why and stop asking how. The hard part will follow, but I cannot help but believe that if we sought the best America we could imagine, it would look very little like what we have today, a country tearing itself apart and racked by guilt, self-hatred, and resentment. That's the win-win outcome we need.

Epilogue: Heartfelt Appreciation

All thoughts expressed above are my own, but I want to thank certain people without whom this book could never have happened.

Firstly, I want to thank my parents, Gerald and Catherine, who passed entirely too early after living a hard life where they gave me the luxury to be a thinker before I learned also to become a worker. With love and teamwork, they taught me the import of family and I miss them dearly.

I want to thank my friends who have followed me on this strange crusade that has become my life. Because I don't want them to become targets, suffice it to say I value all your friendship and the many conversations we've enjoyed. Your encouragement helped me finally put this together, even if it has taken years and there's always room for improvement.

I want to thank the good people of Jackman, Maine. I loved serving you as Town Manager, hope always for a prosperous and happy future, and though some will not realize this, take on this fight so you can stay just as you have always been. The quiet corners of the world exist because some dedicated few fight for liberty elsewhere.

I want to thank my friend Ghost and the entire Inner Circle. Through many laughs and evenings, I've enjoyed our debates and I hope they've meant as much to you all as they have for me.

I want to thank the #GabFam. The last place where free speech is permitted on the internet is worth your exploration and hope you all follow me at http://gab.ai/tomkawczynski. If you like my work and want to support me with more than just words, consider becoming a premium subscriber there. We learn from each other each day as we work to take back what we lost.

There have been several peer readers, most of whom choose to remain anonymous, but know that you have my personal gratitude and with your skill and talents, this book has been much improved.

My eternal gratitude and thanks go to John Young who made this First Revised Edition possible and whose wit, wisdom, and friendship has taken these ideas and presented them in a much more accessible format. Please consider checking out his organization of European Americans United at http://www.europeanamericansunited.org.

I also want to acknowledge the great help, friendship, and patronage of the Boston Boys. You know who you are, and I'm grateful to you all.

I hate to break Rule 1, but thanks both to Halfchan and Cripplechan. May shills be forever damned, but /pol/ will teach you more than any degree if you have but the patience to learn and stomach to listen. One day, it will happen.

Thank you to the shock troops. You've been helpful in every argument and you know who you are, and I'm sure you will be awesome in the future.

Lastly, I offer thanks to Dana, my patient wife and Lyme Warrior. We promised to walk this road together, and even though we've stumbled more than we have run, our steps have become ordered in the light of the Lord and in the good of our people. I could not ask for more.

Keep an eye on www.nationalright.us for what I will be doing next. I have learned in this life that when one door closes, another one always opens if people have only the courage to walk the before them. God bless you all.

-Tom
Easter Sunday, 2018

47670189R00146

Made in the USA
Middletown, DE
09 June 2019